MECHANICAL BULL

MECHANICAL BULL

HOW YOU CAN ACHIEVE STARTUP SUCCESS

CHERYL CONTEE

WITH CONTRIBUTIONS BY **ROZ LEMIEUX**

LIONCREST
PUBLISHING

MECHANICAL BULL

How You Can Achieve Startup Success

ISBN   978-1-5445-1267-9 *Paperback*
       978-1-5445-1268-6 *Ebook*

To the people reading this book, the dreamers, the doers, and the strivers, to those with the giddy up, get up, and go!

CONTENTS

INTRODUCTION

AN ENTREPRENEUR'S SPIRIT

From an early age, I was fascinated by the concept of an office.

My father was a professor at Howard University, and he had an office at home as well as one at the university. While he worked at home, I'd hang out in there watching him do his "cool office things." I'd mimic his office moves, trying to get his attention. I had never seen the office at the university, so I had to imagine where he went during the day and what that office was like.

Each weekday morning, while my father worked at his university office, I went to preschool, where I'd set up an office of my own. I recruited my fellow preschoolers in creating and running a tiny workplace. Of course, most of what we did, we had to pretend. No one was going to give us a stapler, for example, so we had to imagine a block as a stapler. My preschool mindset was "We're going to produce," and our preschool office mostly accomplished a lot of busy work, which is what—I found out later—real office work often is.

I'm pretty sure I was the boss. I didn't know about CEOs or any of that, but there were five or six kids who were working for me. We were working together because girl leadership tends to be about flexibility and flux, usually not as rigid and hierarchical as boys tend to be in their play. But I was still the boss.

While I was running my preschool company, I had a side hustle going too. I had a boyfriend, Stevie, beginning in preschool through first grade. We dated for a pretty long time, even by adult standards. At the end of first grade, one of our daycare supervisors said, "You two have been dating longer than any of us have, so it's time for you to get married." On a beautiful June day, a sixth grader married us. I was very much in love, and we would "kiss," which meant we would stand several feet apart and then lean toward each other, close our eyes, and eventually find each other's face. It was a little precarious, but we enjoyed it.

The other kids found this behavior fascinating and

would ask us to do it all the time during playtime and recess. Eventually, I grew tired of being simply a show for spectators, and for the first of many times to come, my entrepreneurial spirit kicked in. I saw an opportunity.

I told the other kids, "Look, if you want to see us kiss, it's going to cost you."

For big kids, third grade and up, the cost was twenty-five cents. For the younger kids, it was a sliding scale of five to ten cents, or whatever they had. Stevie, being a true romantic, had some moral qualms and emotional concerns about selling our love. I was able to mollify those concerns by buying us candy and ice cream with the proceeds. It didn't make him completely comfortable, but it kept him cooperative in the business.

FEARLESS FROM AN EARLY AGE

The striking thing I remember as an adult looking back on my childhood self is that I was rarely afraid. If a fifth grader rolled up and said, "Kiss," I had no problem looking right up at him and saying, "That'll be twenty-five cents."

On the other hand, I was also bullied. At the time, my family was living in an all-white neighborhood and I was going to an all-white school. The kids in our respective grades were fine, and friends helped protect me, but the kids in the older grades often hurt me and beat me up. More than once, teachers looked the other way. I took it upon myself to learn how to fight, and before long, I'd gotten to the point where I could fend off three bigger boys on my own. I broke a kid's nose with a roundhouse kick. There was a *lot* of blood! Through it all, deep inside me was the strong will to stand true to power. As an entrepreneur, I draw on that will to stand true to power each day. I help other entrepreneurs find their will to succeed and bring great products and services to the world too.

If you're reading this and thinking, *I didn't start a business in preschool. I don't even know what a roundhouse kick is. I'll never be an entrepreneur. I'm already behind*, don't worry. I may have been precocious about business as a child, but I didn't fully learn how to tie my own shoelaces until I was in the fourth grade. And like many girls, when I hit puberty, I lost some of the sheer gumption and badassery of my seven-year-old self. It took time to regain her bravery and power.

Let me tell you something else: although I love technology and found my niche in Silicon Valley, I was never particularly strong in math and science, and I'm the worst coder in the world. I did, however, play a lot of video games. When I heard an internationally famous female leader in tech speak live for the first time, she said, "Most of the female engineers I know played video games as kids." I played Space Invaders, Ms. Pac-Man, Centipede—all of them. My brother and I played Donkey Kong on our Atari 800. I became increasingly comfortable with computer interfaces, although an Atari 800 wasn't quite what we'd consider a computer today. In addition to the joysticks, it had a keyboard.

One day I was bored, and I figured out that we could get into the command prompt of the Atari and teach ourselves Basic—a simple computer programming language. We were just screwing around, but I'm sure that early exposure sparked my desire to be a tech entrepreneur, and I'm grateful for it.

DOCTOR, LAWYER, ENTREPRENEUR?

I never lost my interest in technology, but my parents had other plans. I was encouraged to be a doctor and discouraged from other pursuits. I wanted to be a kindergarten teacher, but my parents, both educators themselves, saw the concerning trends in American education and encouraged both my brother (now a pilot) and me to consider STEM occupations. As far as they were concerned, my future as a doctor, ideally a specialist, was decided.

There tends to be a strong drive toward identifiable, high-income professions for immigrants and minorities. Kids who seem like they might be able to go the distance are encouraged to become doctors or lawyers. If the people who influence them know what engineering is, they might become engineers. Becoming an entrepreneur or launching a startup doesn't even cross the radar.

Christie Chirinos cofounded and was the general manager for Caldera Forms, which creates plugins for WordPress. In fact, the Caldera Forms plugin has been downloaded 1.5 million times and reached the top 0.5 percent of WordPress plugins in the world. Christie started early as an entrepreneur and didn't get much encouragement from her mother. She now works with me as the VP of Technology at my newest company, Do Big Things, and told me her first startup story:

> Entrepreneurship is about community. My first business and business website went live online when I was fourteen. I started offering piano lessons to the neighborhood kids to help fund my own music lessons, which my mother couldn't afford. I often think about how my immigrant, single mother reacted to this. She didn't say, "Wow, you're an entrepreneur!" She said, "You're not going to make a lot of money as a music teacher." Immigrant families don't see entrepreneurship the way that other families do, because immigrants have historically engaged in necessity-based entrepreneurship, not opportunity-based entrepreneurship. Necessity-based entrepreneurship is when people start

businesses because of a lack of other work options—for example, not having a work permit or not being a desirable person to hire because of a language or cultural barrier. To my immigrant mother, there was nothing positive about my piano lessons business, because I was doing it because my family didn't have enough money and because I couldn't get a real job. Shifting immigrant communities' perspective on entrepreneurship to recognize the potential of opportunity-based entrepreneurship to provide financial stability is important. This way, immigrant entrepreneurs will be encouraged and nurtured more.

Part of that tendency is the drive toward safety. There's not a lot of safety in entrepreneurship. Being a doctor or lawyer feels, to many, like a safe profession. You're definitely going to be respected in society, and you're probably going to make money. For many entrepreneurs, especially women and minorities, that concept of "I need a safe profession" is one of the biggest obstacles—what I call speedbumps—they have to overcome.

I crossed my first speedbump in college. I began my studies in biology but left the first class with a deep inner knowing that this was not my destined path. I changed my major to ethics, politics, and economics, choosing to study subjects that were more in line with my interests.

Like many college students, I sought a job on campus

to help cover my expenses. I wanted a high-paying job but also one where I could learn a useful skill. I headed to the library and applied for the job of computer assistant. I had recently set up my own Mac SE (while a male friend watched—I was scared!), so I thought I knew ALL about computers.

I believe I was the first black person, and one of very few women, who had ever applied for that job. The truth is I knew nothing about computers or technology, but the group of computer assistants—the nerdiest of the nerds at Yale—recognized me as a fellow misfit and took me under their wing. I learned all about a new thing called electronic mail, which sounded both dorky and fanciful at the time.

Ultimately, my career ended up being a combination of ethics, politics, economics, and technology, but for the first few years, I had no idea what my path would be. Indeed, the career I now enjoy did not yet exist. I moved to China for a year, after graduating, and when I returned, I found myself immersed in the growing IT sector of Washington, DC. I started to see the rise of the world wide web. At that point, the idea of entrepreneurship became clear to me. I saw an opportunity to combine my nuts-and-bolts knowledge of technology with my love of color and creativity.

GET READY FOR A WILD RIDE

There's no greater feeling than getting your first client or investor. You see restaurant or business owners framing the first dollar or the first ten-dollar bill that they received because that was the moment when their dream was realized. Experiencing the thing that you imagined taking place is such a powerful feeling that it can outweigh the fear of risk and desire for safety.

Success can be a little bit scary, too, because you've stepped from the thresholds of theory into practice, and once you're into practice, a whole new crop of issues arises. People compare the startup experience to the ups and downs of a roller coaster, and while that's a good analogy, the concept of the mechanical bull works better for me, especially with regard to women or minorities launching a startup.

When a man rides a mechanical bull, people look at his stamina and his strength. They don't focus on his outfit or which parts of his body are jiggling more than others. It's not sexual. I've witnessed a mechanical bull in action and seen the energy of the crowd change when a woman was riding versus when a man was riding. When a woman rides, the first thing on everyone's mind is whether or not a titty's going to pop out.

It's the same with startups. The standards are different.

The crowd is waiting for something embarrassing to happen, particularly if you're a woman and a minority. The mechanical bull is the startup, and the only question is "How long can I hang on?"

When you climb on, plan to hold on for dear life because that bull will try to buck you. As different things in your startup environment change, you have to shift your energy, change, or counter with the changes. The trick is to stay on and dismount—exit—gracefully. The vast majority of people get thrown off the bull just as most startups fail. If you want to learn to look elegant and survive a gaze that might be impure or harsh in judgment, this book is for you.

One of our first investors, Drew Bernard, Founding Partner of Impact and Innovation at Upswell, had this to say:

> Over the past fifteen years, I have invested in dozens of startups, served on numerous startup boards, and gotten to know countless entrepreneurs. After all of this experience, I have learned that there are certain personal characteristics that seem to stack the deck in the company's favor. First, it's important to find entrepreneurs who are passionate about the work they are doing and have the ability to overcome often ridiculous odds. In many cases, by the time a nonwhite male entrepreneur has gotten to the stage where I get to have coffee and learn about their startup,

they have had more opportunity to develop the kind of resilience required to get through the hard times and stay humble and productive during the good.

You can do this.

FIND DOORS TO OPEN

A common myth about Silicon Valley startups is that to be successful, you have to wear Mark Zuckerberg–style headphones and a hoodie and code all day and build your own stuff. I'm a living example that you can be terrible at coding and have a successful career in technology.

That said, I encourage you to learn to code. Coding is like learning Shakespeare or algebra: you may not necessarily use it in your daily life, but learning it changes something in your mind. You see what's possible. In the twenty-first century, so many doors are opening. If you don't know there's a door and the door is available to walk through, you'll be shut out. I believe there's a huge amount of creativity out there, but people aren't finding the door. This book is about showing you where the doors are.

This book is intended to be a GPS for launching your startup and a guide for overcoming the speedbumps you're bound to encounter as a nontraditional founder: a woman, minority, or both. Your mileage may vary. I won't give you the day-to-day nitty-gritty like accounts payable and receivable. Instead, I'll help you figure out if you have what it takes to be an entrepreneur, show you what you need to shape your idea, the type of collaborators and partners you need, how to talk to investors—and the type of investors to avoid—and how to make tough decisions so your funding stretches as far as possible.

I asked Roz Lemieux, my longtime trusted business partner, to offer her point of view on the topics I cover. There are three types of jobs: thinking, talking, and doing. If you can do two at the same time, you're likely to be successful. Usually, people are good at thinking and talking or thinking and doing, rarely talking and doing. Roz is good at all the things I'm not, and I am so fortunate to have her as a business partner. Her sweet spot is thinking and doing, and my sweet spot is thinking and talking. We call ourselves "spreadsheet" (Roz) and "jazz hands" (me). When Roz and I first started partnering, I was describing a thing, and by the time I finished talking, she had created a spreadsheet. Together we are a triple threat, and over time we've learned from each other. I got better at doing, and she's become an amazing talker.

Roz is a business natural and proof that you can come from a modest background with a non–Ivy League degree and without an MBA, yet successfully launch and run two companies. If you're willing to work hard and smart, you can be successful. She sees things through a slightly different lens than I do, and her comments—highlighted throughout the book—round out my perspective on the experience of the entrepreneurial journey.

I also spoke to many friends, mentors, and colleagues who live and breathe the entrepreneurial world at all stages of development. You'll find their advice sprinkled throughout the book to help provide more insight into the journey ahead of you.

At the end of each chapter, there are two endnotes:

- **Speedbump:** I point out special challenges that women and minorities may face. These tips are aimed to help you spot challenges ahead of time and get over those humps as quickly and smoothly as possible.
- **Investor Eye-Opener:** I often give insight and advice to investors who are particularly interested in understanding how to support women and minorities in overcoming their speedbumps and optimize their potential to be successful in their entrepreneurial efforts.

Even if you don't want to launch a startup, I want you to be comfortable with your entrepreneurial spirit. You can be entrepreneurial within your organization or eventually graduate to becoming an entrepreneur. I hope you learn something that takes your career, and how you feel about your career, to the next level.

PART ONE

DO YOU HAVE WHAT IT TAKES?

CHAPTER 1

THE ENTREPRENEUR

The first great American dream is owning your own house. The second is creating your own business.

Being an entrepreneur is a very compelling idea in American society. The legend of the person who strikes out on his own, risks big, and gains big—it permeates our culture. People want to admire other people who have been successful in business and imagine themselves in their shoes. In 2016 a US president was elected who many people saw as the epitome of entrepreneurship. Entrepreneurial success is the great American fairytale.

The true story—not the fairytale—is that close to 90 percent of startups fail in the first year. People want to be the successful hero of the fairytale, the Cinderella who becomes a princess, but the truth is success happens for a small percentage. Those who do succeed have certain qualities and a little luck. External conditions often play a role in startup success or failure. Sometimes, it doesn't matter how hard you work or how smart you are if the moment isn't right for the market to accept your idea. Napster, for example, was an idea ahead of its time. We all stream music now. By preparing yourself, you can better your odds of creating your own Elsa (from *Frozen*) story.

"If I could change things early in my career, I would have tried to make sure my job didn't get in the way of my career. What I mean is sometimes the particular job that I had to pay the bills wasn't strategic to what I wanted to accomplish in my career overall, and the goals or priorities of my boss at any time might not have contributed to what I wanted to accomplish personally. Now, I still tried to do a good job, and do my best to deliver for that role. But my nights and my weekends and my lunch breaks and my thinking time were all mine, and while I focused more on how to achieve my personal goals in those times, I would have thought less about appeasing any one particular boss or one particular organization, or trying to maneuver through the politics of one team, and focused more instead on the big picture of what I wanted to accomplish with my work overall. I wish someone had reminded me that my boss's goals for me and my goals for myself didn't have to be the same over the long run."

—ANIL DASH, CEO OF GLITCH

ARE YOU AN ENTREPRENEUR?

Deciding to be an entrepreneur is an emotional leap of faith. In his contribution to the book *30-Second Brain,* Christian Jarrett talks about the latest neuroscience around decision-making. He writes, "One might imagine that successful decision making depends on the rational frontal lobes controlling the animalistic instincts arising from emotional brain regions that evolved earlier (including the limbic system, found deeper in the brain). But the truth is quite different—effective decision making is not possible without the motivation and meaning provided by emotional input." Until recently, scientists believed that we made decisions from our cerebral cortex; in fact, they come from a much deeper and older part of our brain, the so-called animal brain. Decisions made there look and feel like a hunch, an instinct, or intuition. Mechanically, your brain is constantly taking in information and making millions of calculations, essentially grinding it through a black box, and out of that black box pops that gut instinct, that hunch, that deep knowing.

What does your gut say about becoming an entrepreneur? Does your gut say, "Go for it! This is the time, this is the window, this is the idea, these are the people!"? Or is your gut telling you something else? There's no right or wrong answer, but know what you're getting into. If you answer yes to the following questions, you might be an entrepreneur.

Do you have a mild obsession that slightly concerns those around you? Think of Elise Strachan, who created My Cupcake Addiction[1] (#SweetSquad)—a successful blog— by baking amazing, complicated cupcakes and taking photos of them. Do you have that kind of passion? Does your idea keep you up at night? Do you eat, sleep, and breathe it when you're not doing your day job? Are you reading books or watching YouTube videos on your topic?

Are you tenacious? Are you the kind of person who makes a commitment and sees it through to the end? Are you resourceful? Are you the type of person who can make a way out of no way? When Sara Blakely had the idea for Spanx, she wrote her own patent application to reduce the legal fees, knocked on the doors of hosiery mills in North Carolina when they wouldn't take her phone calls seriously, and designed her own packaging.

"I'd also want to let every entrepreneur know that perse-verance is the fundamental common denominator in all entrepreneurial endeavors. Fighting through all the nos, all the naysayers and doubters, fighting through your own doubts, persisting through the near deaths (both early near deaths and later on), and pushing through it all to create something: that is the experience. Embrace that going in, and know that every entrepreneur, across all race and gender and

---

1   https://mycupcakeaddiction.com/en/pages/elise

orientation, has the bumps and bruises and scars to show for it."

—MARLA BLOW, COFOUNDER OF FS CARD, INC.

Do you have strong interpersonal relationships? You don't have to be the most popular person, nor do you necessarily have to have a wide network or a community—although it helps. You do have to be able to communicate effectively with and persuade other people.

Do you influence how people see things? If you don't have at least over 1,000 people in your LinkedIn (or other type of network), you'll probably have a hard time building and sustaining your business. Social networks like LinkedIn and AngelList are where the modern-day Rolodex meets résumé. You know someone who knows someone, and these networks bring you closer to finding that someone who can help you with your business. Businesses are built and sustained on the power of relationships. Do you have strong relationships at church or temple or your kids' school or a professional organization? You may know more people than you realize, and now is the time to optimize and leverage those relationships in new and more powerful ways for them as well as for you. There's power in helping someone, and someone in your network can help you.

Are you willing to go into debt? Are you so passionate

about this idea that you would be willing to take on debt because you believe in it so much? A lot of people would say no, and that's okay.

Are you willing and able to take on the risk of being paid last? When Roz and I founded Fission Strategy, our consulting business and later our startup, Attentive.ly, we had to pony up some of our own cash to make payroll more than once. We paid ourselves back, but being a good business owner often means that you have to pay your people before you get paid.

When an idea connects to all the innate qualities of your passion—the tenacity, the sleepless nights, the commitment—often a business is born. I had three or four different concepts for businesses before I launched the first one successfully. Most entrepreneurs have multiple ideas, which isn't a problem. The goal is to move that idea from ideation to manifestation.

ROZ TALKS ABOUT WHEN SHE KNEW SHE WAS AN ENTREPRENEUR

I started my first entrepreneurial enterprise when I was fourteen, a nonprofit called Flower Children, Incorporated. We had to have 501(c)3 nonprofit status since our purpose was to raise money to buy acres of Amazon rain forests for permanent protection. My parents taught me that if there is something to do, just figure out the most sensible way to do it. If that means doing it yourself, then go do it yourself. There's nothing different about doing that inside or outside of an institution.

When I went to college, if there was a club to join, I joined it. If there wasn't, I started one. When I graduated and started work, I found a job in a city that I wanted and found opportunities to be entrepreneurial and innovative inside of that organization. When I felt like I hit a wall, I left and started doing consulting on my own. For me, it's not about being an entrepreneur but about following my interests and passion and using the vehicles that are available to get those things done.

MAYBE YOU'RE NOT AN ENTREPRENEUR

If making decisions is stressful for you, then being an entrepreneur is probably not a good choice. You have to make a lot of decisions every day, and each of those decisions carries some sort of risk. You know that going in. There are small decisions. There are big decisions. But all of those decisions are made in an effort to improve and grow the business. There's a really good chance that it won't. There's also a good chance that some of your decisions will be bad decisions, and you have to be comfortable with the idea that you are sometimes the cause behind small, or large, failures. Is that something that you're willing and able to take on?

Are you more comfortable having someone else make big decisions? Do you prefer to focus on the practice of what you like doing in your work? Then entrepreneurship is probably not for you. That's a legitimate choice, and it is the choice of most people. They want to understand the minimum and maximum required to do their job and enjoy their lives without worrying about payroll. If you're an entrepreneur with employees, those employees depend on you for their livelihood. Knowing your decisions could impact whether a bunch of people are able to buy groceries for their kids or pay the rent is an awful lot of responsibility.

Are you comfortable with hiring and firing people? Few people like firing an employee and most people feel good about hiring, but some people even find hiring stressful. They can spin their wheels trying to find the perfect person, and there is no perfect person. Usually someone aiming to join your team is not a 100 percent fit, but if you're at 70 percent to 80 percent, that's enough. They can be trained to do the rest.

Firing people is something that most people really dread and fear. Are you strong enough inside to quickly identify whether or not someone is performing, and fire them? Or they're doing great, but you're having a challenge in the business, or you have to take the business in a different direction. Are you willing and able to fire a whole department and take on that weight, knowing how you affected their lives? Those are the risks.

Are you a disciplined self-starter? Would you start working in the morning even if no one was watching you or paying you to do so? Can you assign yourself tasks and follow through on self-imposed deadlines or are you more likely to watch YouTube and then take a nap? Entrepreneurs fly solo for the early part of the journey, and unless you are more like Amelia Earhart than Lena Dunham's character from *Girls*, you may need to be honest about your current capacity for drive and self-propulsion. Hating having a boss is not the same as running a business. Working at home in your pajamas isn't about ease and comfort. It's about the fact that you don't have time to put on clothes because you have been working nonstop. That's your first year of business.

"Three things I would tell my former self: (1) to not manage my time as if I was still working for someone else. Entrepreneurship is NOT 9-5! Entrepreneurship is 24/7! Even sitting on a toilet is an opportunity to work, think, and plan! The taller the empire you are building, the deeper the foundation. It takes DEEP planning and FAST execution...and then you PIVOT. Accept it. The goal will always be the same,

but the route may change. This is 24/7! (2) My business partner and I actually REALLY know what we are doing! Filter advice very carefully. (3) Don't chase rabbits! Hunt the woolly mammoth!"

—VIOLA LLEWELLYN, COFOUNDER OF OVAMBA

You also decide what you pay yourself. You set your hourly rate, if that's what your business looks like, or you set your salary. Of course, it's not 100 percent up to you. You have to have revenue, which depends on what the market is willing to bear and the environment you're in. Ultimately, you're in the driver's seat, which can be scary for a lot of people.

BABIES AND BUSINESS

My friend Kathryn Finney, one of the founders of Digital Undivided (which invests in black-female and Latina-led startups), has been featured in many articles and speaking appearances because of her pioneering leadership. *Entrepreneur Magazine* highlighted her typical challenges as a female startup founder:

> Kathryn Finney, a black female entrepreneur who started the highly successful blog Budget Fashionista, said, "I actually had a (venture capitalist) tell me that he didn't do the black woman thing." Finney, like many others, has run into the discrimination underlying venture capital funding.

Some investors have been quite blatant about the discrimination in the past. *Wired* captured the following quote from an interview with John Doerr, lead investor in Google, Amazon, and Netscape, VC at Kleiner Perkins Caufield & Byers in 2008:

> If you look at the founders of Google, Amazon, or Netscape, Doerr's recorded voice said, "they all seem to be white male nerds who've dropped out of Harvard or Stanford, and they absolutely have no social life. When I see that pattern coming in—which was true of Google—it's very easy to decide to invest."[2]

If you've heard, or you somehow believe, that only men have the instinct or ability to be entrepreneurs, well, that's just a whole bunch of honky-tonk we've been sold. In many West African societies, the women traditionally ran the markets. They were entrepreneurs running their stands, and you know a lot of those women had children.

Seventy percent of American pregnancies are unplanned. Do your best to time yours because timing is everything in business, but it's possible that a blessed event could happen in spite of the best-laid plans of mice and women. You then need to decide where you are in the business life cycle. Are you still at the ideation stage? If so, you may

---

2   Davey Alba, "It's Be Crazy if VC Firms Didn't Fix Their Gender Problem," Wired (May 2015)
     https://www.wired.com/2015/05/ellen-pao-trial/

prefer to hit the pause button and get yourself squared away with that little startup.

Starting a business at the same time I was starting my family would have been challenging. A child is a tiny and intense form of startup, and I needed to really focus on my child, to get him up and running, to be successful there, and to get some sleep. Working sixteen hours a day wouldn't have even been possible when my son was born because there would have never been an opportunity to sleep. But that's me.

You can start a business while you're pregnant. While the baby is still inside you, you still have quite a lot of freedom. After the baby is born, everything changes. Although, almost every woman to whom I spoke among my colleagues said they felt they were more efficient and focused on their work than before having children, and I've definitely felt that too.

Neuroscience backs this up. In *The Female Brain*, Dr. Louann Brizendine points out that the female brain shrinks by about a third during the last trimester of pregnancy—I certainly felt some of the edge taken off toward the end of my pregnancy—but over the six months after the baby is born, all the capacity grows back, and the brain remaps itself. I saw it happen in my business partner. She was amazing before she had a baby. After her first child was born, her ability soared. Her brain realigned, and things clicked into gear. She's full of energy and ideas. For me, eighteen months after my son's birth, I can get a lot done in a day and be very focused. All of a sudden, by the end of that process, there are areas in your brain where you are five times faster on your game. You are a different machine.

Brizendine writes:

> The maternal brain circuits change in other ways too. Mothers may have better spatial memory than females who haven't given birth, and they may be more flexible, adaptive and courageous. These are all skills and talents they will need to keep track of and protect their babies. Female rats, for example, that have had at least one litter are bolder, have less activity in the fear centers of their brains, do better on maze tests because they are better at remembering, and are up to five times more efficient in catching prey. These changes last a lifetime, researchers have found, and human mothers may share them. This transformation holds true even for adoptive mothers.

Brothers, don't get offended. According to Brizendine, the brains of men and people who adopt also change when a child enters their lives, but it tends to be less pronounced. Our female brains are engineered to do this.

LONG DAYS, FLEXIBLE HOURS

Launching a business is very hard work, and not everyone has the appetite or the life circumstances to sustain a startup. When I launched my first business, I worked twelve to eighteen hours a day, every day, seven days a week for the first year until my business partner and I agreed it wasn't sustainable. We both committed to taking one day off a week. We still worked more or less that same number of hours each day, but there was one day on the weekend to take a break.

"Doing a startup means signing up for an emotional roller coaster. No matter how successful you are, you're going to have huge highs and you're also going to have really low lows. You're going to have 48-hour periods where you feel both unstoppable and destined for success and then, within those same two days, you'll also feel completely and totally destined for failure. It's a huge emotional burden of being a founder or CEO, but also, it's just a part of the process and something we all go through. Rather than trying to avoid the ups and downs, one of the best things you can do is just prepare yourself for it."

—BRANDON SILVERMAN, COFOUNDER OF CROWDTANGLE

One of the biggest advantages of being your own boss is having more control over the destiny of your day and how you structure your work. Flexible time management is a huge benefit for a woman. If you have children, it means no one is going to stigmatize you or look down on you for stopping work at 3:00 to go pick up your kid from school. It doesn't mean that you work less, it just means that you're able to take breaks to address other parts of your life. The inflexible work binary, where you are either at work from 8:00 to 6:00 or you're not working doesn't exist. The flow of your work day can look different.

You don't have to ask for vacation days; you can just decide when you're going to take a vacation. Chances are, in the first eighteen months to three years of your business, you are not going to be taking any vacations. You should abandon that hope. Nevertheless, you have the freedom to go on vacation if you can. No one can tell you no. You make decisions about your lifestyle. You don't need approval from anyone except your business partners.

Women, on average, are better than many men at networking, being persuasive, and getting assistance among peers. When you're running a business you've got to talk to a lot of people, and you need a lot of help. Networking skills are a woman's secret weapon. I couldn't have launched my businesses without the community and network of friends and colleagues that I built over my career, and I could not have kept those businesses running if I had not maintained those relationships.

For women in particular, being a parent can impact how

you structure and see the business. It doesn't mean that you can't and shouldn't launch a business and also have a family. It just means that you have to factor in some things that men might not feel they have to factor in. If you've got a baby at home, you may have to consider getting childcare. You're probably going to have to take a couple of hours to tune into your child when you get home. You may have to reduce the amount of networking and meetups you do outside of regular business hours. You may need to make hard choices about travel. That forces you to be very careful and smart about how you're using your time, and that can be an advantage.

TAKE THE LEAP

If you're not still passionate about your idea after reading this far, you probably should hit the pause button. The concept of launching your own business is highly glamorized in American culture. That's part of what's made this country great. When you actually start doing it, it's a lot of hard work, sweat, blood, and tears. Unless you want to literally eat, breathe, and sleep your business every hour of every day for the next year to three years, you might as well just stop. If your idea is one you could take or leave, you might be better off trying to sell it than build a business around it.

"I always looked at failure in such a negative light. It wasn't

until I moved to Silicon Valley for my first startup, Sheena Allen Apps, and noticed how they would celebrate failure. Not because failure was good but more so because failure was one of the best experiences and ways to learn and be better. If something along the journey doesn't work, we take a failure bow, pivot when and where necessary, and keep fighting the fight. "

—SHEENA ALLEN, FOUNDER OF SHEENA ALLEN APPS

I didn't wake up one morning and launch a bunch of businesses. I worked quite a long time before launching my business and had ideas for other businesses that didn't pan out. In part, I relied on my gut for those.

I asked my friend James Slezak, CEO and Cofounder of Swayable, what sparked his decision to leave the *New York Times*—a household-name company that your mother could tell people about proudly—and become an entrepreneur:

> Founding a startup that succeeds is always going to let you have more impact and personal satisfaction than being a small part of a large company. So I thought a lot about three questions: One, your risk tolerance: If I leave, am I OK with the possibility that I'll waste a lot of time and resources and have nothing to show for it? Two, the likelihood of success: do I think our chances of succeeding with this concept are above the odds, and how reasonable is the rationale for that

judgment? And three: what would the next few years look like if I stayed? If the answer to that is anything other than unbridled excitement, you start to think more seriously about the other two questions.

A lot of the concept validation can be done as a side hustle since it's basically about talking to people in a structured way. I held a lot of whiteboard sessions with different people who were interested in the idea and had different experiences to contribute. Some of those people ended up becoming advisors or team members, and everybody contributed in some meaningful way.

There's stability and normality that you know you'll be leaving behind for a substantial period of time, and failure is an ever-present possibility. I trained myself to reach a degree of emotional acceptance of the lowest downside scenarios so that in darker uncertain hours, I wouldn't be paralyzed by the fear.

If you've got an idea and your intuition is telling you it's a pretty good idea, it's time to talk with others about it and test it.

"The best advice that I've been given is that you come from a very different background. You've had a different start, and if you get caught up in how far along you think you should be or where you should be, it will only inhibit your

progress. Focus on what you can control and over index on that."

—STEPHANIE LAMPKIN, CEO AND FOUNDER OF
BLENDOOR, (SPEAKING AT SXSW AND CASE
FOUNDATION'S #FACESOFFOUNDERS)

....

A NOTE ON FRANCHISES AND MLMS

If you don't have an idea but you have the entrepreneur-ial itch, a franchise is a potential alternative avenue to start your first business. You have the support of a big brand, and you don't have to do all of the work of estab-lishing a reputation. The first year to eighteen months of a business is all about revenue and reputation. You've taken some of the risk out because you're relying on the reputation of this larger organization. Often, they have resources and training. You might even be able to get a loan to start your franchise.

While a well-known franchise like 7-Eleven[3], or McDon-ald's[4] carries higher initial investments, you can find a franchise for under ten thousand dollars[5].

Franchise is a form of ownership. Multilevel marketing (MLM) is not. If your friend is asking you to throw parties

---

3   http://franchise.7-eleven.com), Subway (www.subway.com/en-us/ownafranchise

4   https://www.mcdonalds.com/us/en-us/about-us/franchising.html

5   https://smallbiztrends.com/2018/10/franchises-under-10k.html

to help her sell makeup, vitamins, clothes, dishes, or jewelry, or to sell something for her in some way, you may be in danger of getting sucked into an MLM situation that will not help you in the long run. For some people, running an MLM scratches that itch of entrepreneurship but, ultimately, it's not your business. You don't own anything. Women, in particular, and minorities tend to be the most popular target for multilevel marketing promoters. People join multilevel marketing companies and even gig economy companies like Uber or Lyft because of the great American ideal of entrepreneurship. These companies portray what they're doing in the terminology of *be your own boss, run your own show, this is your business.* Unless there's a term sheet, operating agreement, or an article of incorporation with your name and percentage shares in it, that is not your business. Ultimately, your efforts serve to enrich someone else far away.

SPEEDBUMP

For tech startups, the system has been optimized for upper-middle-class white males, although that may not have happened because of racial or gender bias nor was it necessarily the original intention. It happened for a host of reasons relating to American history and socioeconomics, and it's important you understand the nature of the environment you're entering as a tech entrepreneur. You may not have the same connections or networks that others have. You may not have ready access to the same kinds of information. Finding mentors might be challenging. Finding investors might be even more challenging. There are now many women and minorities who have successfully launched businesses, but you may still have to be more persistent. You may have to work twice as hard. You may have to knock on twice as many doors in order to get the same opportunities.

INVESTOR EYE-OPENER

The traditional founder—the upper-middle-class, white Stanford dropout—has invisible, intangible, important resources simply because of his background. He likely comes to the table with resources and connections from friends and family. He may come from a family of entrepreneurs or business people. For the nontraditional, minority, or female founder, you may already be one of the most successful people in your family with few more experienced nearby models on which to tap. Your family and friends are trying to borrow money from you, not the other way around! I'd had success in business and had no idea what was going to hit me, in part because I hadn't seen much successful entrepreneurship in my own family. Most nontraditional founders haven't either. They may even be the first in their family to go to college, let alone have the luxury to drop out. One of my friends told me that his grandmother died and left him six hundred thousand dollars. This gave him the runway to launch his now booming business from his bedroom. This is not a likely scenario for a nontraditional founder who is more likely to be supporting other family members. On top of that, they simply don't have the frame of reference of the startup world of Silicon Valley, even though they're smart, successful people, due to lack of access.

Monique Woodard, a legendary VC (venture capitalist) based in the Valley, travels widely in search of overlooked startup gems. She writes on *Medium*, "We all know that the founders building the most important technology of tomorrow might not be in Palo Alto or San Francisco, but how many of us are getting out to Atlanta, Cleveland, or Kansas City to meet them?"

CHAPTER 2

THE IDEA

There's something contagious about the experience of getting your voice out to the public. In the early aughts, I worked in a public affairs firm in Washington, DC. I was always looking for ways to use technology and digital communications in my job, part of which was to create a relationship between our clients and the newly powerful bloggers. As I got to know political bloggers and activists, a number of them convinced me to launch a blog myself.

At the time, most of the political blogs were written by white men. There were a few popular black political blogs, like Pam Spaulding's *Pam's House Blend* and Terrance Heath's *The Republic of T*. The strongest blogs were run by LGBTQ folks—which was great—but those blogs provided a voice for a subculture within a subculture. Few people were representing the mainstream African-American voice. I saw an opportunity and decided I was willing to give it a try along with my cofounder Baratunde Thurston.

Cast your mind back to 2006. There were fewer black pundits and reporters on the air than today. Media representation of minorities at that time was frozen in a few limiting archetypes: black preacher, led by Al Sharpton and Jesse Jackson; athlete or entertainer, such as Magic Johnson, Jay-Z, and Beyoncé; and the scary black criminal on the news. As a community, African Americans are so much more than that, and no one conveyed the voice of the vast majority of hardworking, taxpaying, middle-class, educated African-American citizens who were trying to get through the day. Gen X and Millennials in particular wanted to break open that narrow paradigm and bring the voice of the hip-hop generation to the public discourse. The internet proved to be the best vehicle and continues to provide greater depth, texture, and complexity in describing the black experience. My blog, *Jack and Jill Politics,* was among the first contemporary efforts in that direction and created an opportunity for hundreds and thousands of voices today.

FILL THE GAP

The *Jack and Jill Politics* blog was born to fill a gap. We set out first to have a black female voice and a black male voice because the experience of black women and black men is a little bit different in American society. We wanted to make sure we were getting both of those voices. We ended up attracting other really great bloggers as well, like Adam Serwer of *The Atlantic*.

My audience for *Jack and Jill Politics*, to a certain extent, was me and people like me. A secondary audience was readers who were curious about what the black person in the cubicle next to them actually thought about the hot topics we covered.

If you see something missing that you or your peers would dig or desire, don't assume someone has invented something to fill that gap already. There may be an alternative out there to what you have in mind, but the thing you design and create meets a need no one else is filling in a better or different way.

"I think that starting with a blank canvas as a new brand was actually one of our biggest strengths when we first launched Away because we didn't set any kinds of limitations or parameters around what we could do, and we were able to imagine and pursue things that might have otherwise seemed impossible."

—JEN RUBIO, COFOUNDER AND CHIEF
BRAND OFFICER OF AWAY

ROZ TALKS ABOUT WHERE IDEAS COME FROM

Frequently, creative ideas are born out of personal experience. You're familiar with a particular problem because you've lived it, and you've come up with the perfect solution. You then need to zoom out and validate that your solution actually works as a business. Do other people with your problem have a budget to solve it? How many of them are there? Is it a big enough market? Will they buy at a price point that makes the investment of your time and money worthwhile? How mature is the competition? Or has a shift in technology opened up an opportunity to solve the pain in a new way? Too often, entrepreneurs don't do the "back of the envelope" math up front on their business idea that investors can do in their heads.

There's a whole genre of thinkers, practitioners, and consultants called futurists, but you don't have to be a trained futurist. You have to be a keen observer who can imagine an alternate scenario. You must be someone who doesn't accept the status quo because, most of the time, new ideas are about doing something someone else is doing, but better.

ROZ TALKS ABOUT A FRESH APPROACH TO EXISTING IDEAS

Some products come to the market before the market is ready. Conversely, products that seemed like a tired or silly idea have been wildly successful. For example, Slack came onto the market *twenty-five years* after IRC and five years after Yammer, with perfectly adequate chat platforms from Google and others in between. Yet it became the fastest-growing startup in history because they took a fresh approach to building the business—using techniques from MMORPG game development (the company's origin) to make the product addictive and then cleverly monetizing well into the customer journey when switching costs are higher. Or Twitter, 140 characters on your phone. Who'd have thunk? It wasn't something anyone thought they needed, but Twitter did it in a smart way, and a decade later, it's still a multi-billion-dollar business.

TEST YOUR IDEA

After you've thought of an idea to fill a gap you see, you want to validate it. At first, this means talking about it. It's fine if the people around you don't have the vision or imagination that you have. If you're a nontraditional founder, there's a pretty good chance the people in your immediate vicinity may not get it. You have to be willing to be vulnerable in a confident way and get out there to talk to people about your idea. Worry less about someone stealing your idea, and worry more about whether anybody will ever buy or invest in your idea. The more people you can talk to and get their thoughts and feedback, the better.

"Find early supporters who truly believe in you, create deep relationships there, and network through that network. While it may still take longer to cross hurdles and get to the finish line, I believe people are waking up and change is happening. If you have a supportive network of the right people (not necessarily a large network but the right people) and an open mind to receive feedback, you can use that feedback to navigate the next phase of business."

—KESHA CASH, VENTURE CAPITALIST AND
FOUNDER OF IMPACT AMERICA FUND

Create a prototype if you can. A prototype facilitates dialogue with people so they can see and touch your idea. You want feedback. The people you talk with help you get your product right before it goes on the market. The feedback also helps you learn to sell your product. If ten out of twelve people you talk to raise an issue about part of your product, it may not be that you're wrong; it may mean that you're not making a proper case. You may be leaving something out in terms of underscoring the opportunity, the target market, or the problem and solutions. Look for what might be missing that can help people better understand the problem and the solution.

"*What this means is that there are SO many ideas and there is so much advice. You will start out with lots to focus on and will get lots of differing pieces of advice. Start the process of narrowing down to the main thing and be comfortable with rejecting advice if necessary. It's your circus and it's your monkeys! You ARE the ringleader of your circus!*"

—VIOLA LLEWELLYN, COFOUNDER OF OVAMBA

If you have an idea but can't create a prototype, try to convey as much as you can of your concept in other formats. For example, you may have an idea for an app, but you're not a programmer. Create a sketch or ask someone to create a rough graphic of your idea. Write it down. Create a list of bullet points that outline the features of the product. The more that you can produce some sort of prototype—even if it's not an actual working prototype—the better the dialogue with prospective customers and investors will be.

MINIMUM VIABLE BUSINESS PLAN

The concept of a minimum viable product (MVP) is still very much in play in Silicon Valley/Alley/Beach. Just as you want an MVP, you also want an MVBP, which stands for minimum viable business plan. (I made up that term just for you, dear reader!) If you're not sure about where your startup fits in the grand scheme of things, filling out this four-square graph may help you. It helps to figure out what kind of business it is in order to map out your strategy for entering the market, i.e., what kind of sales engine might you need? Selling a lot of something low cost to a broad audience is different than selling a little of something expensive to a niche audience. Check this out and find where your business might fit.

WHERE DOES YOUR STARTUP FIT?

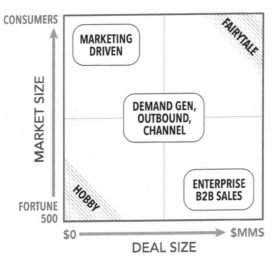

Will your business create consistent *measurable value* for a customer with *spending power* in a large enough *market* to achieve your *business objectives*?

Once you've determined your idea is viable, you can
begin planning how to bring it to life. Nobody reads traditional business plans these days, and a business plan is
time-consuming to create, and in business, time is money.
However, there are key elements of running a business
that you need to think about. Many entrepreneurs are
using a business canvas tool like the one you see below.
The Business Model Canvas was originally developed
by Alexander Osterwalder and visually presents the
nine building blocks of the activities you need to think
about to launch your business. Niche-specific canvases
can be found by searching "business canvas model" on
the internet.

THE BUSINESS MODEL CANVAS

KEY PARTNERS	KEY ACTIVITES	VALUE PROPOSITIONS	CUSTOMER RELATIONSHIPS	CUSTOMER SEGMENTS
	KEY RESOURCES		**CHANNELS**	

COST STRUCTURE	REVENUE STREAMS

You'll then want to translate the information from the Business Model Canvas to your startup pitch deck. If you're able to tell your story and answer the questions a prospective customer or investor will have, you're in good shape. You don't need more than ten to fifteen slides to get started.

Even if it's only you and your partners who see the slide deck, making one is a thought exercise you should go through to validate your idea as a business. You need to think about those questions anyway in order to run a successful business, so while you're answering those questions, you might as well start to shape a deck that you can use for investment purposes. You can use the pitch deck to recruit team members. You can use a version of it with clients, vendors, and suppliers. The pitch deck is something you can use time and again to present your idea.

BUILD YOUR PITCH DECK

You've got your great idea. Let's say your idea is a high-tech shoe for kids that's somehow connected to the cloud that allows parents to follow their child on their daily journey. You build a prototype—you insert a GPS into a shoe and put it on a toddler—and test it out. Then you present your idea and the prototype results to potential partners or investors in a slide deck.

Your deck shouldn't be more than fifteen slides. You want to keep it fairly tight. If you want to see what an award-winning pitch deck looks like, you can watch Jewel Burks's pitch for Partpic (acquired by Amazon) on Vimeo[6]. Generally speaking there are at least ten slides that you need, plus another four or five optional slides.

Those first four slides tie the idea, the problem, the solution, and the audience together:

---

6   https://vimeo.com/145622787

- **The first slide** introduces your vision or big idea. You might have an image of a child at Disney World wandering in a crowd of characters and the parents looking at their phone to track the child. People can see the value of your GPS toddler shoes.
- **Slide two** describes the problem. Here you go a little bit deeper to help people understand the hole your product fills. If you're solving a problem that's for a specific niche audience, in this case parents with small children, you may have to illustrate and describe that problem more fully. While any parent knows it takes a millisecond to lose a child in a department store only to find him hiding in a clothes rack, nonparents might not see the usefulness of GPS toddler shoes and need a little more explanation.
- **The third slide** presents the solution. The GPS toddler shoes offer busy, easily distracted parents peace of mind.
- **The fourth slide** addresses the market. You want to describe your target audience and illustrate how many people have this problem and how much of that market you think you could penetrate. Rough estimates are fine here and are expected. Aim high—big numbers help!

The next group of slides addresses the business model:

- **Slide five** outlines how you plan to make money by

showing the cost of goods and how you'll price the product. Think about whether you'll offer a wholesale or direct-to-consumer price or both. Is this a B2B (business to business) or B2C (business to consumer) product or service? That will impact your pricing model.

- **Slide six** talks about where people will buy your product, for example, online or in a brick-and-mortar store.
- **Slide seven** describes your marketing strategy, where and how people will learn about your product, and how you plan to get your product in front of people.
- **Slide eight** lists your competitors and explains where you sit in relationship to competing options. Compare yourself to the competition and show any traction or current users you have. These figures show you've validated your product. On this slide, you can also reference anything you've learned about your target audience's interest, which could come from surveys or comments on social media. If you've been mentioned in the media, include that too. Anything that validates your idea is helpful to have on a slide. Your business model should address each of these issues.
- **Slide nine** presents the team. To date, you may have been an army of one as a nontraditional founder, but investors want to know that you understand that you're not good at everything (even though, yes, I know and you know you are a superstar!) and that you're going to need a team that brings different skill

sets. You don't have to have all of your team members in place, but to help funding, the slide should illustrate where you sit on the team and show the other team members you'll include. The core team members tend to be the visionary, the tech lead, sales and marketing lead, and some sort of advisor.

- **Finally, there's slide ten,** which asks for the investment. The amount you ask for often depends on the stage of your startup. If you're at the seed stage, the ask is usually in the two hundred fifty thousand to five hundred thousand dollar range. You may have bootstrapped the initial stage and now want to scale, and your ask may be higher. You want to indicate the amount and how you plan to use it. Nontraditional founders tend to be overly conservative in their assessment of where the product can go. Dream big because investors are going to cut it by a third to half, so you want your sales forecast, your cash-flow forecast, and your profit-and-loss statement (P&L) to look exciting. Be hopeful and optimistic.

Beyond slide ten, there are a couple of optional financial slides that are nice to have handy should people start to ask more specific questions. It's a good sign when people start to ask about the financials, and it's helpful to show the hockey stick projection of starting small and growing fast. It's a useful exercise for you to think about your cash forecast over the next three years. Have an optimistic, yet realistic projection of how revenue will grow to a size that can produce a meaningful return for investors. Angels and VCs are used to hearing bloated estimates and tend to discount. You don't want them to discount you out of business right out of the gate. That said, not all business models go hockey stick, and a hockey stick to one million or ten million dollars likely won't justify a five hundred thousand dollar investment.

If you don't know how to do a cash forecast, search the internet or take a guess. It's okay to estimate because it doesn't have to be perfect. People dumber and sloppier than you have been given millions of dollars for their dumb, sloppy ideas. You're smart enough, and if you can't figure out how to do it yourself, then make it your mission to find that team member or partner who can help you on AngelList.

Our first slide deck, like most, was pretty terrible. We did the best we could with the information we had. We put together my pitch deck, and I shopped it around to people I knew, asking if it looked right, sounded right, and if anything was missing. I got a lot of helpful feedback. Show your pitch deck to as many people as possible before you go into more formal pitches. Each time you present your idea, you gain insight and should go back and refine the pitch deck to reflect what you've learned.

Shyness, uncertainty, or an apologetic stance are not

compatible with startup success. You have to be willing to believe in your concept when no one else will. Only then can you convince people to be part of your team.

SPEEDBUMP

When you're solving a problem for black women or for Latinx, there is a chance that problem may not be as big of a problem for many white men. When Katherine Finney, the Budget Fashionista, first presented her groundbreaking business idea, a lot of white males had no concept of what she was talking about. As a nontraditional founder, you may be solving a problem for a particular audience that white, male, upper-middle-class investors have no experience in and, therefore, can't go with you on the journey to imagine that your product would be important. They may be dismissive or demand more information from you than they would ask from someone else because it's not a slam dunk in their mind. One way to overcome this speedbump is to show them the money. Show them the size of the market they're unfamiliar with and how much they're spending today on the crappy competition you're going to crush. I remember watching three enterprising young women from Georgia Tech enthrall a room of investors in describing the sheer billion-dollar size of the "ethnic hair" market. They won their pitch and got the investment they needed.

INVESTOR EYE-OPENER

Twenty years ago, young white males were the ones who were driving tech adoption. Those days have ended. Today, millennials, minorities, moms, or some combination of those three drive the technology that will be adopted. What's more, Michael Lewis wrote on Money Crashers[7], "Despite near equality in numbers, according to Bloomberg, women make more than 85 percent of the consumer purchases in the United States, and reputedly influence over 95 percent of total goods and services purchased. Women as a whole are considered more sophisticated shoppers than men, taking longer to make a buying decision." If you're not solving the problems of the people who buy 85 percent of things and influence 95 percent of goods and services purchased, it means that you're missing the boat in terms of the types of revenue and innovation you can create. You have to reach beyond your own prison of experience in order to get to that next breakthrough app or product or service and reap the rewards.

---

7   Michael R. Lewis, "Men vs. Women: Differences in Shopping Habits &
     Buying Decisions," *Money Crashers*. https://www.moneycrashers.com/
     men-vs-women-shopping-habits-buying-decisions/

CHAPTER 3

THE TEAM

I've never been afraid to put myself out there, which gives me an advantage as an entrepreneur. And I've hit the glass ceiling inside larger corporations. Perhaps that resonates for you and your experience. Many entrepreneurs are driven to create their own businesses to have more control over their own careers. I was passed over for an expected promotion written into my original offer letter as a VP for Digital at a major international public relations firm, despite bringing in hundreds of thousands of revenue, most likely due to gender and/or race bias. I had to make the tough decision to stay or go out on my own. When I took the leap and left my job, I tweeted something to the effect of, "Hey y'all—I'm available for new projects. Who wants to partner with me?" That was a brave and crazy thing to do, but I actually got some incoming interest. See what I'm talking about in terms of the power of a network? I knew I wanted to create and launch some sort of tech startup. I had the passion I spoke of earlier, but I didn't have a specific idea.

WHO'S WHO

Investors—and sooner or later you'll speak to investors if you're launching a startup—want to see four key positions covered in a tech startup: the visionary, the geek, the sales person, and the advisor. One person may cover more than one role, but these are the positions that cover the tasks and responsibilities of a successful startup and are the roles investors want to see you've filled when you ask for funding.

THE VISIONARY AND THE GEEK

Every tech startup begins with an idea and the technical manifestation of that idea, with a visionary and a geek. Sometimes you may be both of those roles rolled into one, but more often than not, you are one or the other. The classic Silicon Valley example is Steve Jobs and Steve Wozniak, who founded Apple. You want a partner who complements you. As you look for partners or team members, recognize your strengths and look for people who have strengths where you have weaknesses.

Are you the visionary, or are you the geek in your company? Roz would say we came up with our first idea together. I believe the seed of it came from Roz.

ROZ TALKS ABOUT COMPLEMENTARY PARTNERS

Look for people who are complementary to you, not just in skill set but in instinct, who are smart and brave about different things. Individually, I was inclined to come up with product ideas, while Cheryl was always inclined to think big about what we were capable of as a team. If you find people who complement you, it really increases your chances of success. Cindy Mottershead, our CTO, brought to the table what was newly possible thanks to advances in technology, like machine learning.

The visionary represents the company and the idea. To understand the difference, the visionary goes to trade-shows and talks to 10,000 people about the product while the geek talks to customers one-to-one via phone or online chats. As you consider your strengths and weaknesses, imagine which of those activities you see yourself doing day to day.

The geek or tech lead, obviously a key role in a tech company, manages the product. Just because you're a technical person doesn't mean that you are the best person to be the tech lead. The geek must be in love with the product itself and want to dig deep into the creative side of the product design and development. The geek works with the developers and designers and talks to customers to learn what's working and what's not working in the product.

Jeff Bezos is clearly a hardcore, all-day-long visionary. However, anyone who remembers Amazon in its early days remembers the concept of buying books on the internet was novel. Amazon wasn't the easiest site to navigate, nor was it beautiful. Bezos recruited talented technologists and tech leads—geeks—whose names we never hear. Someone close to Bezos has been able to help manifest all his great ideas, but that person doesn't want to talk to you. The geeks are working on the products while Bezos thinks about making Amazon more amazing every day.

Mark Zuckerberg, on the other hand, fills the geek and visionary roles as a CEO of Facebook, while Sheryl Sandberg focuses on operations. Zuckerberg legendarily prefers talking to fellow developers, and Sandberg speaks to a different set of people inside and outside the organization. Initially, the visionary motivates team members, represents the company with the customer base, and often ends up being the CEO. Are you that type of person who wants to grow and manage a team and wants to be out front in the public eye? If so, maybe you should be the CEO.

ROZ TALKS ABOUT THE HALO EFFECT

The halo effect is a real issue. Entrepreneurs start businesses that they're passionate about, and they're naturally amazing sales people. Some of them can go out and sell a million dollars' worth of their product, but that doesn't mean that they have a legitimate, sustainable business on their hands. The halo effect can quickly become the horn effect. If you're highly networked or tied to a niche community and sell something you believe in to people who know you or are a couple of degrees separated from you, it's very easy to get a false sense of market validation. There's a strong pull to want to validate the idea quickly, which can be a handicap because it's very tempting to believe those first sales you make yourself are a true indication of the market.

SALES LEAD

The visionary is the key representative for the company and product and will help with sales and marketing, but you need someone who's focused on the audience, on both getting customers and keeping those customers happy. Just because you're a great visionary and are great at describing the product doesn't mean you have any training in sales or marketing, especially if you tend to be a more technical person. The sales and marketing person takes responsibility for how the product is being described in the market. You want to find someone who has experience in sales and can set up a sophisticated sales operation for you. At Attentive.ly, one of our key first hires Artie Patel was able to identify our best potential customers, develop a strong lead pipeline, and describe our product and its impact to those leads in ways Roz and I never could have. Because we are not sales pros!

ADVISOR

Do you know someone who has a few gray hairs in the biz, literally or figuratively speaking? The ideal advisor may cover those gray hairs with their fabulous stylist but has nonetheless been in the game longer than you and has been successful in a related field. You want someone who is willing to be a mentor to you and your startup. A good advisor may ask for 1 percent to 3 percent of your initial returns, and a good advisor is worth it. A good advisor sees around corners that you haven't encountered yet and helps you make better decisions.

We were lucky to find a great advisor in Murray Goldman, an entrepreneur and angel investor active with Atlanta Tech Angels. He was a nurturing and supportive advisor who eventually joined Attentive.ly's board of directors. He was a calming influence who was transparent about his own challenges and how he navigated toward success.

He was always willing to ask probing questions about the business that made us think more deeply and broadly than we might have on our own steam.

Investors want to see the advisor role filled because it shows you acknowledge you don't know everything and are actively seeking counsel to make better decisions. Having an advisor means you have someone around who has more experience and can help prevent big mistakes.

"You desperately need someone who can be 100 percent honest with you. While you also need champions, advocates, and unconditional supporters, it's oftentimes harder to find the people who are knowledgeable about your industry and also feel comfortable enough with you to tell you the uncomfortable truths. Early on in your journey, try hard to find at least one or two of those people and go back to them regularly."
—BRANDON SILVERMAN, COFOUNDER OF CROWDTANGLE

Advisors come in a lot of different forms. Your advisor could be a former boss who has been a successful entrepreneur and now wants to help support you. She could be someone in your network who, again, is more advanced in her career, has created a company, grown it, sold it, or otherwise been successful. He could be someone who emerges as you dialogue with people. A potential strategic partner who runs a firm that's further along than yours could take on the role.

You may clearly state to potential investors, "Frankly we could use an advisor." If you don't have that person within your immediate network, that's okay. Angel investors are often willing to be advisors even if they choose not to invest in you. There are a number of organizations and websites that are basically dating sites that match up entrepreneurs and investors. Check out AngelList, S6.com, or PitchBook.com. The important thing is knowing it's a role you need to fill.

PARTNER UP

You may have a great idea that you've been sitting on for a really long time, and you may feel quite alone. Many nontraditional entrepreneurs start their first venture alone for various reasons. For example, a stay-at-home mom's professional network is not what it was when she was working full time. A younger person may still be building a professional network and doesn't think she has the necessary connections to form a partnership or team.

"As with all things, many narratives were true. My team, Morgan, Jeff, Jonathan, and the other members of the Blavity family are the hardest working people I know. AND we also had privilege, assistance, and incredible support along the way. It makes me wonder, if the hashtag #afrotech ecosystem received even a small fraction of the privilege and support

that white-male-founded companies receive, how many more Blavitys would be possible? We need to support each other."

—AARON SAMUELS, COFOUNDER OF BLAVITY, (POSTING ON LINKEDIN)

In order to find people who share your passion and can get behind your idea, bring it out in the open and talk about it. It's important to create paths to break through whatever your barrier is in order to give your concept the greatest chance of life.

ROZ AND CHERYL TALK ABOUT HOW THEY DECIDED TO PARTNER

Roz: I remember sitting next to Cheryl at an event and her telling me about how she lived in China and does Tai Chi sword. I thought, *This is a cool person I would like to get to know better.* When I heard through the grapevine that she'd left her job at the big PR company, I reached out to her. The next time she was in town, we sat down together, and Cheryl, in Cheryl-style, let me know there were lots of people vying for her attention but that she'd consider it. We agreed to keep our eyes open for opportunities to work together.

That was in the spring. We reached out to our network and let everyone know we were available to help nonprofits with digital projects. We hustled, and by the end of the summer, we had three or four consulting contracts in the works and one active contract. Our first client was Moms-Rising, and today, they're still a client of Do Big Things.

We realized if we wanted to promote ourselves as a pair as opposed to indie individuals, then we needed a name and a website, and that meant incorporating. If we really start taking in money, we've got to get a checking account, etc. In a week's span, leading up to the Democratic National Convention of 2008 (a big networking opportunity for us at the time), we put everything together so we had a business entity to accept the work that was coming in. We scaled from there. We hired people as we needed, and by the end of that year, we had a business.

Cheryl: Not long after tweeting my availability, I saw Roz speak at the New Organizing Institute giant happy hour that she had put together. She spoke on stage and was a flawless badass. I remember thinking, *Wow. I need to talk to her after this. She's pretty amazing.* I knew of her professional reputation, but it was her boyfriend who introduced us. He simply said, "You two should know each other," and left us to chat. That meeting was the beginning of a solid partnership that's lasted over ten years.

Roz had a fantastic reputation, and as soon as we started to work together, it just felt like we were a magical combination of talents that could accomplish anything.

As you talk about your idea and meet people who are interested, get to know them. If someone seems like they'd like to work with you, follow your gut. Don't ignore your intuition just because they have a great résumé or lots of connections. You'll know on the inside whether or not this is the right person. The questions and doubts that emerge from that gut level are usually right.

"I met my cofounder at a startup event. Turns out, networking works! However, it doesn't work the way people think it might when they're looking for a cofounder. I met Josh Pollock at a Startup Weekend event, and we stayed in touch over our mutual interest in web development and running ethical businesses. It wasn't until almost a year after we met that we joined forces as a founder team. We both shared a feeling that the industry that we were both working in as freelance web developers needed better tools and services, but we had to explore our ideas, points of mutual interest, and priorities first."

—CHRISTIE CHIRINOS, COFOUNDER AND FORMER GENERAL MANAGER OF CALDERA FORMS; CURRENT VP OF TECHNOLOGY OF DO BIG THINGS

Likewise, if someone with a thinner résumé seems like a good match, think about how their strengths fill in for your weaknesses. Have they overcome great odds? Are they determined and persistent? Are they super smart or an amazing coder? If part of their experience is thin, look for balancing attributes.

When looking for cofounders, assess their management experience. You don't hear much about the importance of management skills, but a lack of those skills can cause a lot of problems when you begin to grow. At the beginning stages of most startups, there are only a few people, and everyone is doing all the work. Each person manages themselves but no one else. As you scale the company, some people can't transition from building the team to managing the team. If you bring in a co-founder who doesn't have management experience, that's on you.

Look for people who have done the things that they say they've done. Make sure they have relevant experience. Being your husband's third cousin is not relevant experience. Those are two different things. Just because Peanut and Ray-Ray want to work in your company and are available doesn't mean that's a good idea. Peanut and Ray-Ray can find their own jobs without your help.

Every person on your team needs to bring their maximum to the table. Make the best choices you can. Be exquisitely careful in selecting your initial people because each one can make or break the success of your venture.

Jeanette Russell led our marketing at our startup Attentive.ly. She was amazing and now works at Blackbaud, who acquired us as a senior solutions nonprofit marketer.

She believes that working at a startup accelerated her career and says,

> Working for a startup can be an opportunity of a lifetime to develop your skills and confidence by creating a unique space for you to shine. Whether you're a seasoned professional, a recent graduate, or simply feel like your talents aren't aligned with your current job, the startup life allows you to hack and hustle your way to a radically empowering path.
>
> Because each role is critical to the survival of the company, you will be put into a sink-or-swim situation which will test your ability to adapt to the problem of the day. Imagine being a department of one, performing core daily tasks, in addition to finding out about, oh let's say, losing access to a key data stream which happened to be a competitive differentiator...and that's just Monday. It's a wild ride.

Lastly, make sure you like and trust the people you bring on. You are in a startup, it's ride or die, and this is your posse. One of the things that most commonly sinks young companies is infighting among the founding team. To provide a nerdy analogy, you want to form a Voltron—a super-robot that's actually a bunch of smaller robots that create a bigger robot to better defend the universe. You do not want a bunch of robots fighting with each other, messing up Earth like one might see in the *Transformers* movies.

I asked my friend Charlene Li, Principal Analyst at Altimeter and author of the classic *Groundswell*, "How did you find your cofounders and prevent infighting among you?" She said,

> Honestly, we weren't very good at it! They are all good people, but we had a fundamental underlying difference of how we looked at the world and wanted to run the company. We tried to create a core set of values. Although we agreed to them, our interpretation of them was wildly different! The best thing we did was to incorporate feedback, training, and processes, and that helped tremendously by creating a foundation of transparency and trust. That allowed us to put out in the open any disagreements, and when the time came for departures, they were a lot easier because we knew we wanted to do well by each other.

SECONDARY ROLES

New entrepreneurs think they have to work thirty-six hours a day and cover all the roles. The truth is you're not able to do all of these things all of the time. You need specialists to cover some of the secondary roles. Look for creative ways to fill the gaps.

CUSTOMER SUCCESS

Customer success focuses on retention rates, not sales.

Startups tend to fill the customer success role later in the business life cycle, but that person can be a great asset when hired up front. Part of the customer success role is to make sure people are able to use your product effectively. This person figures out what customers like and don't like and conveys that information to the rest of the team, particularly the tech lead and product development. If there's something that's going to prevent someone from staying on the platform or renewing their license, your customer success person will be the first to know. Retention rate is one of the important metrics that investors look for, especially down the line when you reach Series A or Series B funding.

PRODUCT LEAD

This position is different from your geek or tech lead. In an early startup, the product lead is often the CEO and/or the founder. I'd argue all three are "primary" roles in a software startup. Roz and I would advise anyone launching a software startup with a compelling concept, but without a strong software-development background, to hit Pause and take a couple of free courses online via YouTube or elsewhere on design thinking and agile software development practices.

In a well-run software business, you have a triad that works together to determine the product roadmap. The triad consists of project management, software engineering, and user experience (PM/SE/UX), and these three represent the balance between value, feasibility, and usability for your target audience. You need to keep all three components in mind as you build your company, and they intersect as shown in the Venn diagram, which comes from Sam McAfee's article "Twelve-Week MVP" posted on *Medium*[8].

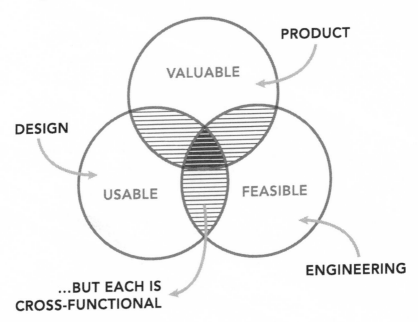

MANUFACTURING

If you're creating hardware or some sort of physical prod-

8   Sam McAfee, "Twelve-Week MVP," *Medium*, March 13, 2016. https://medium.com/startup-patterns/twelve-week-mvp-a24d7739d306

uct—something people can hold in their hands as opposed to something that lives in the cloud or is a service—look for a manufacturing person as soon as possible. You want someone who has both manufacturing experience and relationships with vendors and suppliers.

VIRTUAL ASSISTANT

Rather than hiring a full-time person, a virtual assistant, or VA, can pick up the slack on a lot of administrative tasks so you can focus on being the visionary or geek.

KEEP AN EYE TO THE FUTURE

You start by building your initial team, but if you're successful, those people are going to need to hire people as well. Generally speaking, most people can handle five to seven projects at any given time and manage five to seven people effectively.

You can spend too much on employees and staff, but you can also spend too little. Facebook is a great example. People internally have whispered to me that only when you need seven people can you hire one person. That solution might have looked smart when they were a scrappy startup and before their current problems as a global and powerful corporation. However, at this point, they probably just don't have enough people to keep an eye on all of the things that are happening on the platform and maintain its integrity. Don't hire too many people, but know when it's time to hire in order to continue growing.

One of the keys to success is to find people who are very different from you in terms of personality, experience, and strengths. So much of funding is based on pattern recognition and people who look like you, yet the strength of the team comes from seeking people who are different but complementary. A lot of magic comes from the collective creative persona of different people with different specialties bringing their talents together. Ahem, it's also called "diversity"!

I'm not necessarily a details person, and I know that about myself. I'm a pretty good talker and a pretty good thinker, but I'm not great at actually doing anything. For partners, I look for people who are detail-oriented and who are great manifesters or implementers to complement my strengths with theirs. You may be the kind of person who can take the ball and run with it, but ultimately likes to work with someone who has the flashes of insight and inspiration, which you can then bounce off, take on, and make your own.

Now that you have your idea tested and your team together, you're ready to look for the money to make it happen.

"One of the biggest things I wish someone had told me early on was to really think about playing the long game. That longer perspective changes everything you do—from who you want to work with to even being less attached to any particular idea. For example, there might be one specific idea that seems like it's the most important thing in the world in the present moment, but over the scale of how long it will take to realize your idea, it becomes a footnote. It also means that relationships really, really matter, and everyone you choose to work with is a person you should think about in the full scale of how their career and skills will develop over time, as well as how your trust and familiarity with them will evolve over the course of your working relationship.

In short, long-term thinking is a superpower and one that's easy to get distracted from in the day-to-day stress of building a business. If you can hold on to that bigger perspective, you'll do better in the long run."

—ANIL DASH, CEO OF GLITCH

SPEEDBUMP

Recruiting employees might be more challenging just because people may not initially take you or your concept as seriously as they would from someone else who might look different and come from a different background. Even though it still happens quite often that people create teams that are all white guys, or even all

Asian-American males, people are going to look at you and say, well, why isn't your team reflective of your own diversity? You should practice what you preach in terms of diversity and inclusion, and make sure you are creating a diverse team. That's not just people who look like you.

INVESTOR EYE-OPENER

While being an advisor or mentor to your founder isn't required, it can be an opportunity. If you're an investor, especially an angel investor, you've already been successful in the game. You're still in the game because you love entrepreneurship. Nontraditional founders need your support on the business level. That doesn't mean they want you to come in and run the business, but you can fill the gaps with your knowledge, access, resources, network, and even a shoulder to occasionally cry on. If you see something—in the P&L, product description, beta product UX, pitch deck, the tone of your founder's voice, or their bloodshot, darting eyes—even in conversations, find a way to point it out without being condescending or patronizing. Your guidance can influence whether or not the business is going to make it over that hurdle. Be a supportive ally because your support can make a huge difference. Don't assume someone else will step in, especially since a nontraditional founder is usually tapping a shallower well in terms of allies and resources.

PART TWO

BUSINESS
LIFE CYCLE

CHAPTER 4

BOOTSTRAP OR FUNDING

Nobody's going to leave you a six hundred thousand dollar inheritance to launch your startup. If you're a nontraditional founder, it's just not as likely to roll out for you like that.

The accepted and tolerated concept that you'll ask friends and family for money to get your product up and running is just a non-starter for your average black or brown person. Your friends and family probably don't have money to help you on your entrepreneurial journey. As a technologist, you're likely making the most money in your family. It's a reverse "friends and family" round. People ask you for money.

However, you don't have to be a single parent to your

startup idea. You can find funding if you know where and how to look.

"Think long and hard about how much capital you'll need and see if there is any possible way to make it without raising outside capital. It turns out that raising outside capital is not a success in and of itself (despite all the fanfare and celebration we may hear). It can provide fuel to keep going, but it's not a destination. Taking on outside capital dramatically changes the dynamics of managing your business, and not just for the better. I'd say bootstrap, bootstrap, bootstrap. And then, when you can't bootstrap anymore, only then should outside capital enter the consideration set."

—MARLA BLOW, COFOUNDER OF FS CARD, INC.

SIDE HUSTLE TO MAIN GIG

Roz and I launched our digital consulting company, Fission Strategy, to help nonprofits build movements via social networks. We noticed that our clients were talking to their audiences over email and on social media as if those were two completely different audiences. This practice limited the impact they could have in motivating those audiences to take action, vote, or donate money to a worthy cause.

We saw a gap. Fission had a great tech team, and we built out a tool we called Attentive.ly and tested it internally.

To get started, we pitched our client NRDC on the concept and its potential impact. We charged a rock bottom, nearly at-cost rate of about $27,000 and used that seed money, in part, to build Attentive.ly (shout-out to Apollo Gonzales!). Once we had a working prototype, we asked some of our other forward-thinking clients if they wanted to beta test it. Up until now, we'd offered consulting services to these clients, and now we had a product to offer them. We got a lot of terrific feedback from the clients who tested it.

Most entrepreneurs, especially nontraditional founders, launch their startups as a side hustle. We worked long hours to manage existing clients, our busy existing business, and get Attentive.ly off the ground simultaneously. In the early stages, our product was a side hustle that we worked on in our spare time. We bootstrapped the product development by using excess developer time. When our developers weren't busy with other paid client work, we would ask them to pitch in and help. Developers like to develop and were happy to take on the creative challenge.

ROZ TALKS ABOUT BOOTSTRAPPING ATTENTIVE.LY

We bootstrapped our startups in two steps, which wasn't on purpose but worked out nicely. We started the consulting agency Fission Strategy first. As that matured, it became a third-party entity that could bear some risk. We were able to take some of Fission's revenue and point that toward taking a risk. We didn't have to write checks out of our own checkbooks. The truth is, there was literally no difference between writing the checks to developers ourselves or writing checks from the Fission Strategy account, but it felt safer. Initially, Fission paid for around twenty thousand dollars' worth of development to create a limited prototype that we were able to show around to get some feedback. When we received positive feedback and interest from an initial customer, we realized we needed another twenty thousand dollars to scale it to more than one customer and add more functionality.

If we'd had to write a check for twenty thousand dollars each in one day, that would have felt gut-wrenching. Because we could invest a little bit at a time from the existing business, it felt like a business investment. Part of running a business is deciding how to use the revenue to either pay people more or generate more business. We reached a growing pains moment. When we reached the point of scaling such that the new startup was outgrowing its home at Fission and needed to be spun off with its own dedicated team and sales in order to grow, we began to raise capital.

As clients used the product more, they asked for features we didn't have that we knew would take more time and money to build. Clients were willing to pay for more services related to the product, and as word got out, people asked us if they could become beta testers. We saw a strong appetite for the product. Tools that helped people identify influencers and automated email or social responses that felt natural to the user had been in existence in the private sector for a long time. The nonprofit sector lacked awareness about these tools and techniques, and for those who knew about them, the price point was too high. We were passionate about bringing that technology and that way of thinking about audience to social causes.

The positive response we saw encouraged us to move forward. When people used the product, the results were unbelievable. One of our clients, MomsRising, wanted to run a campaign around toxins in the Northwest. Attentive.ly's software helped MomsRising to find people in their network who were on social media and taking action over email. They then identified who among them were top influencers on social media. MomsRising contacted those people and asked, "We have this campaign, would you be willing to tweet or put up some Facebook posts about it a few times a week? We really need your help." One hundred percent of the people they contacted said yes. Those online influencers were already passionate

MomsRising supporters, and they could reach hundreds or thousands or millions more people than MomsRising could on their own. We saw the power of the software in those results and understood what it could potentially achieve. We believed it could be groundbreaking for nonprofits. Between the positive client feedback and the amazing results from the beta testers, we saw the game-changing potential of the product. The technology worked, and the product was feasible.

As your side hustle grows, you have to determine how much support your side hustle needs in order for it to become your main gig. Part of the challenge with Attentive.ly was managing it within Fission Strategy. We had reached a point where we had to either put Attentive.ly on a shelf and focus on our Fission clients or give Attentive.ly a life of its own with a paid staff and dedicated resources. It was clear that if we were going to get the product beyond beta testers and to a larger client audience, we needed to raise capital. We knew that with adequate resources we could achieve that goal.

We bootstrapped the product internally at Fission for eighteen months and then launched, but within the first six months we knew using excess Fission developer time wasn't sustainable. We could see that the side hustle that became Attentive.ly would need its own budget and its own team.

VENTURE CAPITAL

I started the fundraising process and was the lead fundraiser in the first round. (Roz was instrumental in subsequent funding rounds.) I ran a successful consulting company. I was a technologist. I thought being a tech entrepreneur was an extension of those roles. The world of tech startups is different. It has its own rhythms, roles, and rules. Don't assume that you know what you need to know simply because you're involved in technology. Startups and funding are a subculture of the tech world that's worth boning up on. Read as much as you can when you're starting out. Read Eric Ries's *The Lean Startup*. Watch the first season of HBO's *Silicon Valley*. It's broad and satirical, but everything that happened in the first season happened to us.

As you begin to talk with investors, you'll hear and see different levels of investment discussed. While the age of the company is a factor, the level of investment you require determines the type of funding round you seek. Early stage and late stage are general terms. Early stage usually means seed or friends and family stage and covers funding up to five hundred thousand dollars. Series A and Series B tend to be between two and fifteen million dollars and focus on developing the business. A well-developed company asking for Series B funding could be considered late stage. Series C or D funding can run into the hundreds of millions of dollars as the company prepares for an acquisition or an IPO.

There are a lot of different types of funding vehicles. You should educate yourself on different types of equity, like convertible notes versus preferred stock versus common stock versus stock options.

Jewel Burks, founder of Partpic (acquired by Amazon), started her career at Google but was inspired to take the startup leap by her grandfather. She took a leap of faith and moved from Silicon Valley to Atlanta. *Forbes*'s 30 Under 30 profiled her on YouTube[9]. You can look it up and get inspired!

She was working at a parts distributor, and her grandfather called her from the family farm in Alabama asking for help to find a part for his broken tractor. He figured since she worked at a distributor and knew about Google, that she'd be able to help him. Try as she might, she struggled to find the part online, and she was seeing the same challenges among her company's customers. Partpic allows people to take a couple of photos of a part that needs replacing, automagically finds all the relevant and key information, and helps you locate that part online. Cool, huh? I asked her to look back on her fundraising journey:

> The thing I would do differently if I had to do it all over again is to understand the mechanics of VC math before I started fundraising. I wasted a lot of time with funds who

9   https://www.youtube.com/watch?v=hIp4dB9wXoU

could never invest in me because the amount I was raising did not align with the check sizes they write. Having a better understanding of how and why VCs make the decisions they do would have been very helpful, and it's something I highly recommend to founders I advise now. Knowing what I know now, I would have focused more on nondilutive capital such as SBIR (Small Business Innovation Research, www.sbir.gov) and NSF (National Science Foundation, www.nsf.gov) grants given the heavy research component of Partpic.

Ours was a young company even though it had been around for eighteen months, and we had some customers on the platform. Investors distinguish between pre-revenue and post-revenue companies. Some people believe it's easier to raise money pre-revenue because you're still in the realm of theory, ideal, and dream, even if you have a working prototype. Once you are post-revenue, when people are paying for your service or your product, you're facing the messier details of customer success and recurring revenue. The challenges that you're facing are much more vivid and apparent.

Part of the reason to bring on an investor is you're looking for more than money. Investors own a part of your startup. They have a vested interest, meaning they also share the financial risk. Often the investor can fill the advisor role on your team when you're first starting out.

HELPING YOUR CHICKS HATCH: INCUBATORS AND ACCELERATORS

Incubators and accelerators can really speed up the process of going from an idea to reality.

- An incubator tends to be a very early stage when you are working through the concept of your business. You may not have a prototype or team yet, but you're on your way. The incubator is intended to be a concentrated period in which you can begin to put meat on the bones of your business.
- An accelerator supports a business that may be pre-revenue but has at least a prototype and a team. At this stage, the business is ready for the next stage of development, and an accelerator connects you with more mentoring and more funding opportunities.

Both can be very helpful to businesses, but for nontraditional companies, participating in either can be challenging, especially if you have children or an existing job. Both incubators and accelerators often require founders to travel and live in another city for three months or more. Hubert Zajicek, CEO and Cofounder of Health Wildcatters, in an article for *Entrepreneur*[10] wrote, "Most startups can benefit from an incubator when they're trying to get their business model together and go from

---

10   Hubert Zajicek, "Accelerator vs. Incubator: Which is Right for You?," *Entrepreneur*, May 26, 2017. https://www.entrepreneur.com/article/294798

concept to reality, but not everyone needs an accelerator." Incubators don't provide capital, but they provide other support. Accelerators are about funding and most ask for a share of equity in return for very strong support. It's a trade-off. Entering an accelerator can be a huge deal, but you do give up something in return. Incubators are more about helping to build your confidence and your ability as a founder to take next steps.

Many incubators and accelerators exist, and I strongly suggest searching online and applying. The most famous accelerator is Y-Combinator, which has been a game changer for many companies.

If I had my way, there would be far more incubators and accelerators, particularly ones that address nontraditional founders. They need to be in rural areas and the Midwest, not just Silicon Valley, Silicon Alley, and Silicon Beach. To transition the economy to the information age, accelerators and incubators need to be accessible in communities in need, i.e., where car plants are closing, so people can begin to transition to a new way of working. Good ideas can happen everywhere, and the best ideas come from places most impacted by the changing economy.

ROZ TALKS ABOUT ACCELERATORS AND INCUBATORS

Early on, I proactively hired engineers of different genders and age groups. When the time came to raise money, one of the vehicles for that was accelerators. At the time, they all required everyone going and living somewhere together, dorm-room style, for three months. I had employees who had teenagers, and I had a baby. We weren't in a place where we could just up and leave our families for three or four months, so that door was closed to us because of who I was and the phase I was in my life but also because of who I gravitated to hire.

So much has changed since 2012. Several funds, and new ones every day, are focused specifically on female founders. I was able to join an accelerator that was just for female founders and met in person without requiring everyone to live on-site. There's always been a layer of cheerleaders for us, people who help female-founded businesses all along the journey, including our first investors. And the good news is that there's a lot more now than there were five years ago.

ALTERNATIVE FUNDING

We focused on venture capital because that's what was available almost a decade ago. Today, you have several options to launch your startup.

STEWARD OWNERSHIP AND DEMAND DIVIDENDS

Steward ownership works for companies that want to do something for society beyond maximize shareholder profit and sustains the idea that the people making decisions for the company should be the ones who run it, not a board of directors or outside investors.

Max Slavkin, Cofounder and CEO of the Creative Action Network, describes this experience in his article on *Medium*[11]:

> We started structuring the deal as a convertible note, because that was literally the only way we knew you could structure it—we'd never heard of a startup at our stage doing anything else. We knew it wasn't a perfect fit, that a convertible note only "converts" upon a future financing event or exit, and those weren't things we ever wanted to do. But it was something we could ask people to sign, and just getting people to say yes seemed hard enough without trying to do anything nonstandard.
>
> In the first three months, after about forty-five meetings, we had just three people say yes, but at least we were on the board. We connected with Purpose Ventures, a new firm based in SF and Germany who liked what we were doing and, more importantly, introduced us to a novel model

11   Max Slavkin, "Our Alternative Journey to Alternative Finance," *Medium,* July 23, 2018. https://medium.com/@TheCreativeAct/our-alternative-journey-to-alternative-finance-6216e6fa909

for companies like us who needed capital and wanted to stay independent. The ownership concept is called steward ownership, the idea that companies should exist to do something for society beyond maximizing shareholder profit. It's a fairly commonplace notion in Europe (and throughout American history) and that the people making decisions for the company should be the ones running it, not a board made up of outside investors.

And they backed that idea up with an investment model that was based not on future speculation, but on capped dividends (sometimes called Demand Dividends). Once we hit a certain revenue threshold, we start paying a portion of our profits back to our investors, until they've all received five times their initial investment. That solved the "exit" problem and meant investors can make a solid return without CAN ever being sold. Finally, we'd found a way to raise money that actually reflected our goals and our values.

Their commitment pushed a few more angels to our side and brought our total investment round to $380,000—thirty thousand more than the goal we started with! But more than the money, we had a financing structure that actually aligned everyone's incentives: When CAN makes money, our artists make money, our nonprofit partners make money, our investors make money, and most importantly, more social-impact artwork is created and distributed. There's no pressure of an exit looming to distract us from the real work of the business. We're focused on our artists, our customers, and our impact, not on the hopes of a bigger future deal. And with a five-times return, our investors are still poised to make real money over time, without pressuring us toward unreasonable scale or away from our mission.

FINTECH LOANS

There are definitely more financial vehicles to help you get up and off the ground quickly than when we were starting. Don't get a payday loan to cover your startup costs. You want to be smart about the type of funding you use, and the good news is you don't necessarily have to max out your credit cards or get a home equity loan. Particularly for that initial seed funding, startup financial tech, or fintech, companies have emerged to meet the needs of small businesses and fledgling founders. We used a fintech service to help patch a few holes when we were having cash flow challenges in our company.

NerdWallet.com lists resources for business loans, some of which you can obtain online. Fundera.com, Street-Shares.com, and Kabbage.com offer resources as well. You don't have to wait twelve months to get a venture capital investor if you tap into one of these fintech options, which give you a boost while you're working on obtaining investor funding.

Make sure you read the fine print about the type of guarantee needed before you sign those loan papers. Chances are you will struggle, and you don't want to lose your house if you're not successful. Seek legal and accounting advice about structuring your company properly. Consider setting up a C-Corp so you're working with money that you can declare bankruptcy against and get relief from the debt.

At some point, you're going to need more money than these types of services can provide, depending on what you're building, but they can help you bridge the rough spots.

SWEAT EQUITY

While we were testing Attentive.ly, we were approached by CrowdTangle to invest in the launch of their product. They were bootstrapping, using friends and family funds and some of their own resources to get the company off the ground. Fission Strategy had a good reputation for technology. We had the resources they needed. They wanted to work with us but explained that, given their startup status, we were expensive for them. We believed in their product, but we had to keep a roof over our developers' heads. We worked for them from the start for full price, but when their seed money ran down, we agreed to keep working at cost and replace our profit with sweat equity, meaning we earned equity in their company as we helped build the product.

Sweat equity can be a great way to make investments. If you're a woman, you're black or brown, or all of the above, the amount of sweat equity you can provide might be limited because you may have less disposable time and income. Other people may be depending on you, so sweat equity may have a higher cost.

Consider sweat equity but be careful about the terms. You don't want someone to take advantage of you. You want to be a team player, but you also need to look out for your own interests and make sure you're being treated fairly.

No one's going to give you what you don't ask for. Ask for a term sheet that defines what your sweat equity means and spells out what you receive in exchange and when. If you're providing sweat equity while waiting for funding, if you're still in the side hustle stage and you're working as part of a team, how will you be compensated or reimbursed for some of that labor once you get funding? Make sure you're covering your costs and getting something in return because, again, most startups are going to fail. Calculate the cost of your sweat equity if the company fails. Of course, you want to calculate the upside too, but you have to think about the risk management.

ROZ TALKS ABOUT OPTIONS FOR COVERING COSTS

Covering our costs was the key for us. We had business assets (developer time) that were sometimes idle and costing us money. The CrowdTangle deal covered our costs and provided a possible future upside. Another benefit was our development team really liked the work, so it kept them engaged.

Our Chief Technology Officer, Todd Kamin, ended up moving over to CrowdTangle as the product began to take off. At that point, we had enough shares to have a vested interest in the success of CrowdTangle. This is a great example of investors providing more than money.

CROWDFUNDING

Crowdfunding is in some ways a more democratic, although certainly more difficult, way to get funding. According to the 2017 report *Tackling the Gender Gap*[12], written by the US Senate Committee on Small Business and Entrepreneurship, women have been 32 percent more successful than men in raising capital through crowdfunding.

---

12 Senator Jeanne Shaheen, "Tackling the Gender Gap," *U.S. Senate Committee on Small Business & Entrepreneurship*, 2017. https://www.sbc.senate.gov/public/_cache/files/2/5/25bd7ee9-a37b-4d2b-a91a-8b1ad6f5bd58/536DC6E705BBAD3B555BFA4B60DEA025.sbc-tackling-the-gender-gap.december-2017-final.pdf

The folks who have had the most success tend to make physical products that people can buy. Crowdfunding is driven by the idea that someone gives you money and if you reach a certain amount of money, you send a product to everyone who contributed. Unless you can reasonably make that claim, it's probably not an option for you. Things may change in the future, and crowdfunding for software-related products and services may become a more viable venue for investment.

You have to have something pretty hot in order for crowdfunding to bring the investment you need. You can't just put something up there and hope. You can't just build a better mousetrap and hope that mice are going to wander by. That's just not how this works. Your product has to fill a need, and you have to network and socialize it.

The foundation of successful crowdfunding is your network. Crowdfunding begins with friends and family, and we've established that as a black or brown founder, the funds that crowd can share are few and far between. If you have three to four thousand Facebook friends and many thousands of Twitter or Instagram followers, then crowdfunding might work for you because you already have a network of people who are interested in you and what you're doing. If you don't have a strong network yet, it's going to be a different hustle for you. Finding angel investors, an incubator, or an accelerator to get started might be more viable. Crowdfunding platforms include Kickstarter and Indiegogo.

ICO

Chrissa McFarlane, Founder and CEO of Patientory Inc., a healthcare data management app, started her company with an initial coin offering (ICO). If you know the right people and know what to do, you could get a lot of funding in a relatively short amount of time. When you approach angel investors or venture capitalists, you're speaking with a few people. With an ICO, you speak to many people. Hundreds, thousands, even tens of thousands come onboard for your ICO. ICOs can be risky, and there is increased regulation being applied to cryptocurrency.

Now that you know the type of funding to look for, let's take a look at how to meet with those investors in the next chapter.

SPEEDBUMP

Startup conventional wisdom will tell you the first funding round takes six to twelve months. If you're black, brown, a woman, or all of those things, it might look more like twelve months for you. It might take you longer, and you may need to knock on more doors to find the investors that get it and/or you. You need to plan differently than someone else who may get more rapid acceptance in the marketplace more quickly. You have to plan for those six to twelve months financially and emotionally to keep your product and dream alive until you get either the first funding round or subsequent funding rounds.

INVESTOR EYE-OPENER

As an investor, keep that very stark difference of beginning resources in mind as you meet the black or brown founder across the table from you. For most black and brown startup founders, there is no "friends and family round" available. Set aside the notion that the nontraditional founder can pass the hat around and receive a few hundred thousand dollars. Consider the following data points that are representative of study after study on the economic racial divide:

- In Boston, the average white family has a net worth of $247,500 while the average US black family's net worth is eight dollars; Caribbean blacks' average is twelve-thousand dollars; Puerto Ricans' average is $3,020; and Dominicans have an average net worth of zero dollars—not a typo.[13]
- The Institute for Policy Studies reports in *The Ever-*

13   Ana Patricia Muñoz, Marlene Kim, Mariko Chang, Regine O. Jackson, Darrick Hamilton, and William A. Darity Jr., "The Color of Wealth in Boston," *Federal Reserve Bank of Boston, Duke University, and The New School,* March 25, 2015. https://www.bostonfed.org/publications/one-time-pubs/color-of-wealth.aspx.

Growing Gap[14] from 2016 that it will take black families 228 years to earn the wealth that white families hold today.

Give your nontraditional founders a break. Show that you have trust and confidence in them. You want to trust your founder knows the market and has a valid business plan and, at the same time, not assume they know everything and don't need help. Lean in a little bit harder and challenge your own assumptions about what amount of money they're asking for. You might think it's a pretty good deal and invest immediately at a relatively low number when it might be smarter to invest a tiny bit more up front, knowing that this business might be undercapitalized and might have a stronger success if you invest with strength early so that they have the best chance to succeed.

---

14 Chuck Collins, Dedrick Asante-Muhammed, Emanuel Nieves, Josh Hoxie, "Report: Ever-Growing Gap," *Institute for Policy Studies,* August 8, 2016. https://ips-dc.org/report-ever-growing-gap/

CHAPTER 5

INVESTOR RELATIONS

One of the best tips I received from one of the VCs I spoke with was, "If you are looking for money, ask for advice. If you want advice, ask for money."

Take that attitude when you go into meetings with investors. Take that attitude in all your communications, including the cold emails or cold LinkedIn messages you send. If you ask sincerely for advice, counsel, and mentoring and explain why you've chosen that person, many people will be willing to help. It's simply polite. People in the investor community are going to find a "give me the money" attitude rude. The best angels are people who see themselves as being able to provide you with more than money.

I spent time sharing the pitch deck for Attentive.ly for feedback and tweaking it after each conversation. Once

I had a decent deck, I felt ready to knock on doors and ask people to connect us to investors they knew. Don't be shy about asking for connections. Mine your LinkedIn contacts for people who can make introductions for you.

We wanted to have those deep conversations with investors. We spoke with Google Ventures, and funding from them would have been amazing, but it was a fantasy. We sought professional feedback on our business model and pitch, and we asked for connections to other investors. Most of what we received from the investors we spoke with was feedback and connections, which was a good outcome because it was information that propelled us forward. When someone connects you to someone else who can help you move to the next level or help you take the next step, that's a positive outcome.

ROZ TALKS ABOUT NETWORKING

Meeting with angel investors is often a means to an end, which is to make the connections and build the relationships that lead to the right person introducing you to the right person to find the initial investor or set of investors. It's not about winning a pitch competition. Even that is only the beginning of the conversation.

Pitch competitions are an excuse to get you in the room

with investors and shortcut the conversation because they're busy and a lot of people want to talk to them. You want to sort the field quickly to get in front of the right person. Some investors are interested in investing in women-owned businesses. Some are interested in B2B. Some are interested in B2C. Some are interested in particular markets like healthcare or ed-tech. Figuring out your profile so you can then find the investors who are interested in that profile comes with experience. But the more conversations you have to build your network, the sooner you'll identify the appropriate investors to approach.

PITCH YOUR IDEA

We cast a wide net in our search for investors, particularly in the beginning. Today, investors tend to be more specialized about the type of investments they make. Look online for angel investors or venture capitalists who might be interested in the type of product you have and the level of funding you seek. For example, in the early stages, look for VCs who do seed rounds and target them. Review the VCs' websites and portfolio of companies in which they've already invested before approaching them to learn about the types of investments they tend to make. Some focus on early-stage companies and seed rounds while others look for Series A and late-stage companies.

If they're interested in doing the type of funding you want, then look at the sector or type of products they invest in. If you focus on software as a service and you pitch a group that tends to focus on hardware, those people are not likely to invest in you. They might not even give you a meeting, but if they do, be realistic about what you can gain from that meeting.

In our case, we sought investors who were, first, interested in software as a service; second, interested in social enterprise and causes; and third, interested in nontraditional founders. We didn't limit ourselves if they didn't have all three. Many investors would focus on one or two of those, but at the time, it was hard to find investors interested in all three.

ROZ TALKS ABOUT TALKING TO THE RIGHT INVESTORS

Going in as an entrepreneur, you may feel like you are blindly asking for money, but that's not what's happening. Investors manage an investment portfolio. If you have a savings account and a 401(k), so do you. From the investor point of view, your startup is an investment vehicle. Investment vehicles represent different asset classes. Those asset classes have different risk-reward profiles. Bonds are low risk, low reward. Early stage startups are high risk, high reward, i.e., they represent a *very* slim chance of making a *lot* of money. Angel investors may have other personal motivations: fun, a desire to give back. When you meet with an investor, research or ask about their other investments. Understand the types of startups that fill this piece of their portfolio. Then think about how the asset that you've created—not the product that you love but the *asset* that you've created, the whole business—would (or wouldn't) fit the investor's portfolio strategy. As you need to be customer-centric in your product development, you need to be investor-centric in your fundraising.

If you're talking to the wrong people, you can miss the cues. If you're looking for five hundred thousand dollars and you're talking to institutional investors, they can say all kinds of nice things to you, and it's meaningless. There's no way they're going to invest in you. A big part of having effective conversations with potential investors is making sure you're talking to investors that are *investing in the type of asset that you have to offer.*

We looked at our network and saw people launching products in the nonprofit space. We told ourselves that those guys—and they were all guys—weren't smarter than us and that we had a good product that people seemed to want. At the time, I didn't consider that I was a black woman entering a white man's space. My only thought was that we had an idea as valid as others that were being funded, so we should be able to receive funding.

"Founders can avoid some of the tiring effort of trying to convince nonbelievers and really focus their energy on building a solid business and attracting those investors who believe in them and the business model and will be value added. The last thing anyone wants is to become a token investment in a portfolio and then get ignored by the investor. Take your time to find the right investors and people who believe in the vision and are there for the long haul. Don't chase name brands. Seek out investors who genuinely want to support you and have the cultural competence and expertise to support you."

—KESHA CASH, VENTURE CAPITALIST AND
FOUNDER OF IMPACT AMERICA FUND

IGNORANCE IS BLISS

I was fortunate that I didn't know how rare it was for black female founders to get funding of any kind. I saw myself as a technologist, like anybody else in Silicon Valley, with a good idea for a product. I had a certain amount of microcelebrity from my days at *Jack and Jill Politics*, which had been a popular blog, and from television appearances. Fission Strategy was a successful, ongoing concern and had experienced millions of dollars in revenue. I felt I was qualified. I was used to people returning my calls and responding to my emails.

Having to be persistent with people to even get a response was discouraging at times. When I finally got in the room, getting people to watch a demo was challenging. My impression was that people didn't believe that I had a real product that was worth their time. I once met with an angel investor contact who was working for, believe it or not, an organization specializing in diverse founders. He vetted ideas before presenting them to the actual investors. He sat through the demo politely and at the end said, "This is interesting software. I can definitely see where this could make a difference. I just don't know if you are the person who can actually take this product to market." He said this to my face.

At the time, I could only assume that race or gender or both influenced his comment because I knew that I had as good of a track record as anybody else walking through that door. We had a good product and paying customers. The group he was part of was dedicated, at least in their mission statement, to helping folks like me get funding. He told me he thought it was a good idea—not that it was a bad idea or that it wasn't a worthwhile product—but that there was a problem with me. The clear, explicit statement was that if someone else had brought it in, maybe it would be okay.

I kept my composure and said, "Okay, it's fine if you don't get it. I believe in this product, and we're going to find the folks who get it, but thank you for your time, and if you know anyone that you would recommend, we'd be glad to talk to them." I just shut it down. It was clear we couldn't expect much from that group.

My instincts might have been to give him a roundhouse kick in the nose as I had to the playground bullies in elementary school, but the Silicon Valley investor community is small. All the investors somehow seem to know each other, although this is changing as the pool of investors grows and diversifies. Nevertheless, you don't want to alienate anyone unnecessarily. It's okay to call someone out, but it's also in your best interest to thank them for their time, stop the meeting, and leave.

"Call out every harasser and cut them off from the get-go: once you accommodate a shmuck—regardless of perceived power—it only leads to greater shmuckdom."
—HEATHER GOLD, CREATOR OF *THE HEATHER GOLD SHOW*

My business partner and I talked about it. For half a second, I wondered if I had to hire a white guy to represent our product to investors. We fought doubt that we'd ever get funding. We took a deep breath and agreed we and our product were as good as the others looking for funding. It took us longer, and we had to knock on more doors, but we found the investor who got the product, got us, and funded us.

"Because the investment world is so demographically homog-

enous, my sense is that most investors simply don't relate to people who don't look like them or founders who are solving different problems than the ones they're used to seeing over and over. So the "pattern recognition" investors are so used to deploying fails them when faced with founders who break the pattern.

Ultimately, we moved forward with Attentive.ly because of how absolutely thoroughly Cheryl and Roz understood their target customers. Attentive.ly wasn't serving a hypothetical need but rather a need that had come up time and time again in the context of the consulting work Cheryl and Roz had been doing."

—CHRISTIE GEORGE, EXECUTIVE DIRECTOR
OF NEW MEDIA VENTURES

Sometimes even if you have a great idea, people, including investors, will dismiss it because you're the messenger. The same idea presented by an upper-middle-class white male to another upper-class white male might be received in a different way.

What's more, conventional wisdom says men tend to be overconfident and overblown in pitches, way into the so-called moon shot category. Therefore, investors in their mind calculate a 20 to 50 percent reduction in the funding they'll provide, whereas women tend to be conservative, modest, and humble. (Sorry, taking a break to roll my eyes.) The problem is investors take that modest, conservative, realistic estimate and cut it in half. Men need to dial it down a notch, and women usually need to dial it up. In order to get to a decent level of capitalization, such that you can be successful, you've really got to talk to that moonshot level.

As you talk to investors or prospective customers, you might get some of that. Don't waste time on people who can't go with you on that journey. If their imagination is that narrow, they're not going to be a good adviser or investor anyway. As quickly as possible, assess if the person in front of you is serious or not, and if not, just keep knocking on doors.

ROZ TALKS ABOUT BIAS

There's a lot of a kind of subtlety to who gets money and which relationships get formed. There's a gut instinct component, part of which is pattern recognition. Potential investors and partners think, *Who do I feel comfortable with? Who looks like the last person that I made money from?* The nontraditional founder doesn't fit any of that. Investors tend to gravitate toward people who fit their profile of an entrepreneur. When we started down this path five or six years ago, people would talk openly about pattern recognition and signals. They looked for people who looked like other people who had made them a bunch of money. For better or worse, neither Cheryl nor myself look like Mark Zuckerberg. That meant potential investors not only needed to like our pitch, they often *also* needed to check their own bias about who makes a successful startup founder.

Today, no one will openly admit they discriminate against founders on the basis of gender and race, but five years ago that was a thing that people said out loud. Thanks to a lot of work by a lot of people, the bias has been shifting radically, and there are now many more investors looking for the next Jennifer Hyman of Rent The Runway or Janice Bryant Howroyd of Act-1 Group.

Another challenge is that success often lies in the ability to take risks at those moments when opportunity arises. "It takes money to make money" is, at least in part, about this ability to jump on a potentially risky opportunity when it arises. So every bit less cushion one group has than another—thanks to historical gender or race bias—inhibits their ability to take those initial risks and snowballs into more and more lost opportunities over time. For us, having Fission to provide that cushion and enable that risk-taking behavior made all the difference.

MAKE THE KEY CONNECTION

Not long after that meeting, we met with Christie George at New Media Ventures, a growing angel network dedicated to social enterprise, particularly in the progressive space. Christie George took the time with Roz and me to help us understand the world of startups and investing. She was frank that Attentive.ly wasn't ready for New Media Ventures, but she introduced us to Kesha Cash.

Kesha was then running the fund for Josh Mailman, who led investments for Serious Change, an early stage impact-driven investment fund. Kesha was immediately excited about our product. She explained how we should brush up our pitch deck and agreed to show it to Josh because he was looking for companies like ours. That meeting was the turning point. We wouldn't have gotten there without the referral from New Media Ventures, who invested in subsequent rounds. Everything came together at that point. Kesha was the guiding hand we needed.

Kesha walked Josh through our pitch deck, and then Josh and I met at the Social Venture Network conference, which he had founded twenty-five years prior and which focuses on furthering the movement of social enterprises. I approached him and mentioned that I knew he'd seen our deck and expressed interest in talking with him further. It was challenging to pin him down, but when he was ready, we ended up sitting on a park bench outside the conference venue for two hours. We talked about my background, his background, my dreams, his dreams, the product, the potential, the space, and what investing in us could represent for other investors and nontraditional founders in the future.

Josh says today, "The idea of looking at emails and social media together to communicate with donors and supporters made sense to us. Attentive.ly focused on next-gen web strategy and opinion makers. From a societal perspective, Roz and Cheryl were doing something potentially transformational in the space. We were also excited to back two female entrepreneurs who were impact-driven and focused on social media at a time when it would make a difference in how nonprofits approached their work. We're happy that the investment made money! More than that, we've found that entrepreneurs of color and women are underappreciated as founders, tend to be more interested in making a positive difference beyond the bottom line with their startup, and thus, make great investments."

WHAT INVESTORS LOOK FOR IN YOU

I'd been working and waiting almost twelve months to have that conversation with Josh. Everything you do from the time your idea is a seed in your mind to building the prototype to reaching out to investors ideally leads up to a meeting like the one I had with Josh. What I understood in hindsight was that, at the seed stage, investors are investing in you, not necessarily the product or service. Angel investors are, more often than not, people who have been successful in business already, and they see qualities in you that you may not see. Because of their business experience, they also know the product or service will change, and they want to see qualities in you that assure them you'll be able to pivot with the product or service. When you enter the marketplace, there will be friction between your product and what people actually want, which leads you to make significant changes in your business model, your product, your target market, or all three. Investors are interested in your creativity, resourcefulness, resilience, persistence, and your ability to make fast decisions and go the distance to win.

"I wish entrepreneurs would talk more about their unique qualifications, experiences and support that will make them a winner instead of acting as if there's absolutely no competition. There will always be someone on your back vying for what you've accomplished, but your persistence and unique approach will be the winning recipe if you always acknowledge that your idea alone is not enough to win. Execute with an innovative and relentless spirit."

—LAUREN MAILLIAN, IMPACT INVESTOR
AND AUTHOR OF *THE PATH REDEFINED*

I asked Kesha, who is now a leading Venture Capitalist and Founder of Impact America, what she looks for in early seed stage companies and why she thought we were a good match. She said,

> Impact America invests in companies who have already received seed funding (post-seed) and you can find the criteria on our website (ImpactAmericaFund.com). Of all of these criteria, I focus heavily on the savvy, scale-obsessed, socially conscious aspect. All of the founders we invest in want to be large businesses and have a successful exit one day, but a passion and mission to make society a better place to live is what drives them to wake up and manage the ups and downs of startup life each day. When I met you and Roz way back when in 2012, it was clear that you two were two extremely smart and business savvy women who were not only committed to building a successful business, as you had already demonstrated through your agency, but were also genuinely passionate about social change based on a number of indicators (your previous work, your political blog, etc.). And while I wasn't as familiar with the nonprofit fundraising space, I am very familiar with the magic of passion, and I bet you and Roz's passion would be the fuel that kept you two going through the tough times, and you'd figure out the rest.

Perhaps you remind them of themselves when they started out. Part of the reason they want to be an angel is to give back and help others the way they were helped. Angel investing is a way for them to stay in the game and continue to participate in entrepreneurship.

"Bring your whole self, and your whole founding team, to the conversation. As an investor, I want to get to know you. The most important indicator of the success of an early stage company is the founders. In order to make an investment, I need to trust your judgment and expertise. I want to see that you have a team that balances each other's strengths and weaknesses. Share your story, your passion, and your experience as well as your business model."

—BETSY HOOVER, COFOUNDER OF INVESTMENT
FUND HIGHER GROUND LABS

Granted, their motives aren't entirely altruistic. They're also making a speculative investment that could potentially yield lucrative results, although their money would be safer in a mutual fund pinned to the S&P 500. They don't have to invest in your company.

When an investor meets you, he or she is doing due diligence on you. They are evaluating your values, your potential for success. They're envisioning a trajectory for you and your product. The investor wants to trust you on a gut level to do something good with his or her money and communicate in a transparent way.

"Not a single one of [potential investors] gave us the RIGHT advice. They all told us what they THOUGHT we were supposed to be doing to protect their capital, but it was misaligned with the size of our vision and our uncanny gut accurate instinct for our market and what the business could be. This time around, we are selecting investors with a much more choosy, discerning approach."

—VIOLA LLEWELLYN, COFOUNDER OF OVAMBA

ROZ TALKS ABOUT CONNECTING WITH INVESTORS

Cheryl definitely struck a chord with our first investor and connected with him on a personal level. I came in and created some confidence around the numbers and business model and did the regular reporting. It's hard to have all those pieces in one, first-time entrepreneur. We were able to play off each other, and we've both become stronger in the areas that we weren't naturally drawn to by seeing it in the other person. Individual entrepreneurs can get burned out because they try to be all of those different things.

An investor signing on, particularly at that seed round, knows—even if you don't—that they'll have to provide more funds to fulfill the promise. They're making a commitment to you, not just in that moment but also to subsequent rounds, without saying so or committing on paper, however. They know at least that they're going to be asked. As you go to subsequent rounds of funding, the level of ownership for initial investors is diluted unless they provide more funding. It's important to understand that you and the investor have a long-term relationship.

"I would have made sure that after the first raise, that I leveraged the buzz and raised (again) RIGHT afterwards with no hesitation."

—VIOLA LLEWELLYN, COFOUNDER OF OVAMBA

Keep in mind, no one will believe in your product more than you. Investors and customers look for your confidence. We were ride or die for our product. And I prayed for help. I'm relentlessly optimistic. A tough meeting or attempt to get a meeting might temporarily get me down, but I pick myself back up. There's a power pose called "goddess arms" or "victory arms," where you stretch your arms over your head in the shape of a V and breathe deeply. In her book *Presence: Bringing Your Boldest Self to Your Biggest Challenges*, Harvard Business School professor Amy Cuddy writes about the neuroscientific research that shows how this stance has a positive effect on your brain. Cuddy writes: "Body-mind approaches such as power posing rely on the body, which has a more primitive and direct link to the mind, to tell you you're confident." I certainly feel it. I still do goddess arms before a tough meeting or before speaking to pull in that positive energy! I recommend it highly—confidence counts.

WHAT TO LOOK FOR IN INVESTORS

You want someone concerned about the health of your business. You want someone who can keep their mind clear to focus on the opportunity, the business model, the revenue, the recurring revenue challenges, and the future of your company.

Similarly, you want an investor who is transparent and trustworthy. You want to understand their motives for investing in you, your product, or your service. You also want to consider what they can provide beyond money. For example, an investor may have expertise in your field and be a great advisor or be able to provide connections to clients or other investors.

"The same advice that my mother always gave me—'The truth shall set you free.' In choosing investors, think, 'Can I always tell the truth to this person?' As no one can help you if they don't have the full picture. Bringing people into your reality allows them to support you—hiding failures only leads to self-doubt and despair."

—MORGAN SIMON, FOUNDER OF CANDIDE GROUP AND AUTHOR OF *REAL IMPACT: THE NEW ECONOMICS OF SOCIAL CHANGE*

As you sign up your first investor, you're also looking for someone willing to be the lead investor. The lead investor is a key role because, psychologically, people like to join. Your lead investor demonstrates social proof for you and your product and draws in secondary investors.

Unless you are fortunate enough to have friends and family who can support you, which is unlikely if you're reading this book, you will have at least two investors in the beginning, maybe more. The initial investor might lead, but they want other investors to join. We had two investors for our first seed round, one large and one small, but the psychological impact of both investors was the same. Our investors were successful entrepreneurs themselves who said with their investments, "We believe in you. We believe in you so much that we're going to put our money where our mouth is." Their confidence in us propelled us forward. The class of investors will grow over time in subsequent rounds. In our case, our initial lead investor participated in subsequent rounds of funding.

SHOULD YOU WEAR A WEDDING RING?

Women experience different challenges in society than men, and one place it shows up is how women are perceived. Investors will make snap judgments—unconscious or not—about you when you're sitting in front of them. Bee Shapiro of the *New York Times* and Ellis Brooklyn was frequently asked, "How are you going to manage everything? How will you balance your personal and professional life?" One day before going to an important investor meeting, she forgot to put on her wedding ring, and the questions didn't come up. So she stopped wearing it to take the question off the table, as it had become a distraction in the pitch. I doubt male entrepreneurs get this question very often.

"When I was raising my first round for my clean-luxury fragrance line Ellis Brooklyn, I found that because I didn't have prior experience running a business nor did I have finance experience that I really needed them to see me for me. That meant thinking of and eliminating distractions. I didn't completely change the way I looked, but I did little adjustments. I certainly dressed a bit more conservatively than I usually did in the sense that I watched the necklines and hemlines. I also showed up to every pitch relatively dressed up and polished. I do think physical impressions matter no matter what people say. It's human nature to assess the physical first, and being a minority first-time business founder, I knew I already had the chips against me. I even took off my wedding ring because I found some of the chitchat during pitches wandering to if I had a family and if I could handle it all. I hated that question most of all because with the success of Ellis Brooklyn and trajectory that we had proved out, questioning whether a founder can handle it all felt antiwoman. I'm obviously handling it all...next!"

—BEE CHANG SHAPIRO, FOUNDER OF ELLIS BROOKLYN

On the other hand, Ariane Goldman, of HATCH Collection, is transparent about being a married mother because it's core to her business concept. She develops and sells high-end maternity clothing and accessories for moms and babies. Letting investors know she's married with children gives her legitimacy that she understands the audience segment because she is the audience segment.

Venture capitalist Monique Woodward counsels entrepreneurs to bring their full selves. Wear whatever you normally wear, cool and funky, classic and preppy, and don't change who you are. You want investors who really get you. Investors who lead your first round may lead your second and third rounds, so you want people who will stick with you and not be surprised as you evolve.

Nontraditional founders often ask if they should bring a white man with them to pitch to investors. If there's a white guy who's legitimately part of your team, then, of course, bring him, but be prepared for the consequences. Some investors may only talk to him, even if you're in the room. I'm sorry to say more than one female founder has had this experience.

The bottom line is don't be dishonest. Don't bring a white man to your pitch meeting because you're afraid that you won't be treated fairly or that you'll be discriminated against. If you're the lead founder, be proud of that.

You want the kind of investor who sees your promise and invests in you specifically, even if that means you have to knock on more doors to find an investor who believes in you, and your idea, all the way. Shortcuts only lead to trouble down the road. When the investor finds out the truth, it will undermine their trust in you, and if there's one thing you need from your investor, it's their trust and respect.

JUST SAY NO

Clearly, you don't want an investor who wants to gouge you and take more of your company than seems reasonable for the amount of investment they provide. If an investor is asking for more than 20 percent of your business, make sure they're bringing something important to the table. The ownership percentage an investor receives should be in proportion to the amount of support and leverage he can provide. If, on the other hand, you're on *Shark Tank*, the sharks are bringing so much in terms of resources to support you, their request for a larger percentage can be justified.

From a financial standpoint, you want to set the valuation of your company as high as possible and keep the great percentage of ownership so you—and your business partners—are the largest shareholder. As you go to second and third rounds of funding, your share may be reduced.

Ideally, you're building a bigger business and increasing the valuation with each round of funding, so while your shareholder percentage may decrease, your gains stand to increase. There's a difference between owning 70 percent of a one-million dollar business and 30 percent of a ten-million-dollar business.

If the investor is spending time with you because he wants to be the CEO of your company or install his own CEO, think twice about taking his or her money.

If the investor is spending time with you because he wants to get in your pants, that's an investment you don't want. You may be tempted and think, *I like tapping that booty*. Booty and investments don't mix. An investor who is focused on what's in your blouse rather than your pitch deck is not making clear and coherent business decisions. They're not focused on the product and the service, they're focused on, again, getting in your pants, and that will be the driving rationale for all of their behavior going forward. And that's a distraction you don't need.

ALPHABET SOUP

During my first investor meetings, I got lost a few times in the alphabet soup. The investors threw around acronyms like a volleyball—NB, MRR, AR—and they went over my head. Pretend like you know what they're talking about and then Google it when you get to your car after the meeting. That's how you learn. You can always say, "That's an interesting point. I need to crunch some numbers and get back to you on that," if you don't have the slightest idea what they're talking about. Just smile, nod, and look confident.

In the meantime, here's a cheat sheet to get you started:

ACRONYMS TO KNOW
AP—Accounts Payable
API—Application Programming Interface
AR—Accounts Receivable
ARR—Annual Recurring Revenue
ASP—Application Service Provider
AUM—Assets Under Management
B2B—Business to Business
B2C—Business to Consumer
BOD—Board of Directors
CAC—Customer Acquisition Cost
CAPEX—Capital Expenditures
CLTV—Customer Lifetime Value
CMS—Content Management System
COGS—Cost of Goods Sold
CPA—Cost per Acquisition
CPC—Cost per Click
CPC—Cost per Conversion
CPL—Cost per Lead
CRM—Customer Relationship Management
CT—Cap Table
CTA—Call to Action
CTR—Click-Through Rate
D&O Insurance—Directors and Officers Insurance
EBITDA—Earnings Before Interest, Taxes, Depreciation, and Amortization
EPS—Earnings per Share
EV—Enterprise Value
IPO—Initial Public Offering
IRR—Internal Rate of Return
ISP—Internet Service Provider
KPI—Key Performance Indicator
LLC—Limited Liability Company

LTV—Lifetime Value
MoM—Month over Month
MRR—Monthly Recurring Revenue
MVP—Minimal Viable Product
NAV—Net Asset Value
NDA—Non-Disclosure Agreement
NPV—Net Present Value
PaaS—Platform as a Service
PPC—Pay per Click
QA—Quality Assurance
QoQ—Quarter over Quarter
ROA—Return on Assets
ROE—Return on Equity
ROFR—Right of First Refusal
ROI—Return on Investment
SaaS—Software as a Service
SAFE—Simple Agreement for Future Equity
SEO—Search Engine Optimization
SMB—Small to Medium Business
SWOT—Strengths, Weaknesses, Opportunities and Threats analysis
TM—Trademark
TS—Term Sheet
UI—User Interface
UX—User Experience
VC—Venture Capital / Venture Capitalist
WOM—Word of Mouth
YTD—Year to date

KEEP INVESTORS INFORMED

In the early days when you've just received funding, you should be head down, nose to the grindstone, working your butt off. Your investors understand they may not hear from you for a while. However, within the first quarter, you should touch base and let them know how things are going. Share the good news and highlight your successes, milestones you've hit, or people you've hired, and ask for input or help if you need it.

Investors want to be informed. Much like a mutual fund

manager or publicly traded company will send quarterly and annual reports to shareholders, investors want to know what's going on with their investment in you. At Attentive.ly, we released fairly lengthy, quarterly conversations, whereas CrowdTangle released short, comprehensive monthly updates. Frequent contact gives you an opportunity to ask for help more often, help that is not necessarily money. Frequent communication keeps investors involved and allows them to participate in your entrepreneurial endeavors.

Some investors want to be more involved than others. Don't worry, they're not trying to run your company for you. Your investors are professional people who are busy doing their own work. It's up to you to leverage the potential of your investors and ask for help. Many of them will tend to lean back unless they see the wheels are falling off the bus or unless they see mismanagement in some aspect.

When you do need help, look through the background of your investors to see who knows what and who might be able to help you with what. When you write your investor updates, be honest about where you're struggling, mention that you're looking for developers or need someone to help you think through your pricing model—whatever the issue is. Someone on your list may be able to help you or know someone who can. Your transparency builds confidence in investors, and those who missed the prior round may be watching you to see if it makes sense to invest in a subsequent round.

You'll have investors who support you from the beginning and others who decide to invest later. Don't assume that someone who said no in the beginning will say no again later. For example, New Media Ventures declined to invest in our seed round, then invested in our Series A. Keep a list of people with whom you've spoken during your funding journey. You might make two lists: one for investors and one for noninvestors, although, to a certain extent, you can send similar messaging to both groups. Include people who weren't willing to take a meeting for whatever reason but provided feedback on a phone call. Stay in touch with anyone who was supportive in any way.

"This will likely not be your last round. You should think about how long this capital will last and what milestones you will need to hit to raise your next round. Don't worry if this seems too hard—a good early stage lead or advisor may be able to help with this."

—JOSEPH THURAKAL, SENIOR PORTFOLIO MANAGER OF TIGMERA (AN ANGEL IMPACT INVESTMENT FUND)

Some founders who skipped the prior round view cheerful, successful emails as a sort of "middle finger" to people who dissed them. If that's what motivates you, go for it. Sometimes those early naysayers may come on later as investors if you play your hand right. Remember, the investing community in Silicon Valley is small, everyone knows everyone, so it's smart to keep people informed along the way.

Make the relationship with your larger investors a human relationship to the extent they're open to that. Grab lunch with your investors from time to time. Ask for their advice. These are smart, accomplished, successful people with heart. Treat them like that, and you'll be surprised how they're going to treat you.

"Think of your investors as another sort of customer for your business. Companies are a multistakeholder model: you have customers, your team, you, society at large (don't pollute please!), and the investors. They are all important. Many first-time founders don't think about investors as a customer with both economic and noneconomic reasons for engagement. You'd be foolish to try to run a business without thinking deeply about your team and your customers. Think of investors the same way (and while you are at it, care for society and for yourself!—I know, easier said than done)."

—JOSEPH THURAKAL, SENIOR PORTFOLIO MANAGER OF TIGMERA (AN ANGEL IMPACT INVESTMENT FUND)

ROZ TALKS ABOUT SENDING
IN THE CLOWNS

One of the most impactful experiences I had pitching investors was at Venture Atlanta, one of the biggest venture conferences in the Southeast. It's very selective and a privilege to be included. They pick the slate six or seven months out. When we got picked, I was pregnant. We didn't want to turn it down because it was an amazing opportunity, but by the date of the event, I was nearly forty weeks pregnant.

At the time, in 2014, very little venture money went to female-founded businesses. The South tends to be more traditional, and Atlanta, where the conference was held, is all about business-to-business, the farthest thing from hipster. Everything about this pitch was terror-inducing.

Founders go through a series of pitch reviews with up to ten investors each. After the first pitch practice, I changed my pitch based on the feedback I'd received, removing a slide or two. At the second pitch practice, the investors asked for the slide I'd removed after the first practice. I received conflicting feedback from different investors at each pitch practice. I was nervous about my increasingly pregnant self and my confidence was plummeting. When the day for the final practice came, Cheryl happened to be in town and asked if she could watch the practice.

I didn't want her to see how bad I was doing, but her advice afterward hit home.

Cheryl said, "The problem is not the content of the slides. The problem is that no one believes that you believe in the product. You're overexplaining and you're under-confident. The world is a stage, and your job is to send in the clowns."

There's no way you can explain the entirety of a business in ten minutes. All you can do is try to plant a seed with an investor that you've got something important that's going to change how things are done. You've got something that's worth their time and attention. I went home and replaced every slide with a picture. I revamped the pitch to connect with investors about a common problem that everyone has and really plant that seed of excitement that what we were doing was different, worth paying attention to, and could potentially be really big. And I added a joke at the beginning about being pregnant. Imagine a thousand investors in the auditorium of the Georgia Aquarium, a sea of gray hair and gray suits. I walked on stage forty weeks pregnant in my teal-blue maternity dress with red jewelry (our logo colors) and said, "Hey I'm Roz, I've got two startups. One of them is eighteen years pre-revenue, so I'm going to talk to you about Attentive.ly."

> It woke everyone up. Understand that all the world's a stage, and your job is to send in the clowns. Get their attention and use difference to your advantage. Make them look at you, make them laugh. I spoke to eleven investors that day in one-on-ones. They all had positive feedback. I also felt I'd done my little piece in providing a different pattern to recognize in the future.

WHEN THINGS GET SERIOUS

It's all talk until there's a term sheet. If an investor seems like they're serious, it's okay to ask directly if they're ready to invest to support your product or service, and if so, if they're willing to prepare a term sheet.

"The best advice I ever got when we were building BlogHer, Inc. came from Caterina Fake, cofounder of Flickr (and then Hunch and Findery).

We were considering a Series A investment and had a couple of irons in the fire. Many people thought Caterina and her cofounder had perhaps sold Flickr to Yahoo! too soon and missed out on a bigger payday, but she encouraged us to assess our options prioritizing People-Terms-Valuation in that order.

What she meant was that, first and foremost, make sure you are partnering up with people who you want to work with every day, people you trust...and who trust you.

And then taking a look at terms versus valuation, don't be seduced by a super high valuation and take on terms that are so onerous or weighted in favor of the other party that you end up never getting a fair piece of that valuation. At the end of the day, you want to feel like the outcome was fair, and you'd much rather have a fair share of a more modest value than no share of a big one.

We ended up applying this People-Terms-Valuation prioritization not just to investors but also to other kinds of partnerships. We wanted to do good business with good people, and this advice helped keep us in the right mindset to do so."

—ELISA CAMAHORT PAGE, COFOUNDER OF
BLOGHER, LATER ACQUIRED BY SHEKNOWS

The term sheet is where negotiations get real and put into writing. At this point, you need an attorney if you don't have one already. Do not assume that you can look at a term sheet and know what's in there. It is worth your time and money to have legal counsel review the term sheet. If the term sheet goes well, then you start to move to the shareholder agreement, and then the process moves quickly. Within a few weeks, not more than a couple months, money gets wired into an account, and you're ready to go.

"I would have also put an equity clawback clause into the equity contract related to lack of support or any other con-

dition that would cause a slowdown in growth. It happened to us and was COSTLY! VCs get away with a lot of garbage behavior."

—VIOLA LLEWELLYN, COFOUNDER OF OVAMBA

SPEEDBUMP

There is good money and there's bad money. Especially if you're a woman, that's a real issue. Be clear about your boundaries and be vigilant. Just because someone has given you money doesn't give them any other rights over you that aren't in the shareholder's agreement. Don't stand for investors who want to leverage their investment or put pressure on you in any way later.

INVESTOR EYE-OPENER

Set up a call to talk with your nontraditional founder. Not only do they want counsel from you, they may need it more. They probably have challenges they're facing that you could help solve by brainstorming with them. There are lots of ways for you to use your network and your experience, beyond financials, to help a young entrepreneur who's coming from a different background than you. Make your investment real and understand that this person may need more support—slightly more financial support but, more importantly, more moral support, more business support, more technical support, more networking connections, and more sales support. Connect them with other resources, such as an incubator or an accelerator, that can give them an extra boost. Don't assume that your founder knows of the places that they can turn to become better business people.

"Cold hard logic: survivorship bias. In order for folks who are considered minorities to make it to the founder level, they have to overcome significant institutionalized hurdles. They are the best of the best to get to this stage. You'd be a fool not to fund a diverse team. A key trait for a fundable entrepreneur is grit. We need to fund people who can stick with a startup. Before I invest, I need to believe you are willing and capable of working at the same insanely hard task for ten years. In some ways, this is the hardest, highest bar for investment. My money would be on these sorts of groups to go the distance."

—JOSEPH THURAKAL, SENIOR PORTFOLIO MANAGER OF TIGMERA (AN ANGEL IMPACT INVESTMENT FUND)

CHAPTER 6

SPENDING WISELY

On HBO's *Silicon Valley*, there's a multi-episode arc of an entrepreneur who gets a bunch of money and blows it on a giant party on Alcatraz Island. Don't let this be you. When Roz and I received two big checks from our initial investors, Serious Change and Drew Bernard, our first thought wasn't, "Great, we've got $375,000 in the bank! Let's go buy BMWs." And it shouldn't be your first thought either.

Getting the first funding absolutely tests your strength and character as a person. Think about the kind of person you are when the first check hits your bank account. Are you the kind of person who's going to take that money, start to giggle, and go on a spending spree at Nordstrom, or are you the kind of person who can fulfill and manifest the dream that you and your investors had together and get to work on that?

Don't be the co-founder who buys a Ferrari with the seed money. And if you have a partner who does that, buy them out now while buying them out is pretty cheap. Or ask them to return the Ferrari because that's not what that money's for. Buying a Ferrari means that you probably aren't going to hire an engineer or a sales team member that you need. Wait a hot minute before you buy that Ferrari. If you do it right, there will be plenty of Ferraris in the future.

We could have taken Serious Change and Drew's money and run to Mexico. If you want to blow your money on some stupid stuff, no one is going to stop you. It's up to you to use those resources wisely. It might seem like a lot of money, but you're not rolling in it. This isn't free money. You're taking money from someone who believes in you and your product. You've entered a relationship built on trust. The way you spend the seed money is an important test of your character.

FOLLOW YOUR PLAN

More than once, I've seen infighting sink young companies in that first year to eighteen months. Friction happens when the founding team has conflicting values or can't agree on the division of labor. The company can't reach a level of forward momentum because the principals can't agree on what they're doing, why, and what their priorities are. They get stuck spinning their wheels, and it's a death spiral for their startup. Nothing burns the runway—the amount of time your money will last—faster than conflict between founders.

The day you receive the money should not be the first time you think about how you'll spend it. It's important to make sure that you've got a full program in place. If you've got your prototype and your technology is getting closer to market-ready, your sales team starts spinning up. If you're ready to start selling, you have marketing and media. You have operations to make sure you're compliant with rules, regulations, and taxes. Of course, someone, probably you, has to be in charge of the financials. All the pieces are critical to making sure your business is going to last, and you have to work together.

During the funding stage, investors will ask questions about how you plan to use the money. However, the conversations with investors tend to be high level and limited to who you'll hire and what you'll focus on. The time to start making detailed plans, if you haven't already, is when you're close to getting that funding. You want to hit the ground running. If you've got a term sheet or you're talking about getting a term sheet, things are starting to get real. Begin to put together a budget and a plan, not only for how you'll spend the money—money that, again, is not yours but your investor's money—but also how you'll know that your money is being well spent, that your business is working.

KEEP AN EYE ON YOUR BUDGET

The burn begins as soon as you receive the funds, and the money never lasts as long as you think it will. You've got to have the maturity and self-control to behave appropriately. Ideally, you have created a plan for the money because now the real work begins. You need to be ready to make quick, often daily, decisions that are sometimes tough decisions.

Work out a budget and figure out how long your runway is; that is, how long will your seed fund last to keep the business running until you're in the black (or can raise more capital)? In the best of worlds, the money lasts your first year, which is a critical time for a startup. Spending it down to get to your next milestone makes things acute. Having customers extends your runway quite a bit and gives you more time to make mistakes. But if there's no money coming in from paying customers, the seed money is all you have and is potentially finite. Consider how you would treat the money if you knew you weren't going to get more. You would treat every dime as if it were a precious, precious jewel. That's not to say you should be miserly. The money is there for you to use, but I see far more people overspending than underspending.

"I rarely talk about this anymore, but when we started Blavity Inc., we didn't make any revenue for the first two years. With very limited investment capital, Morgan DeBaun and I were always looking for ways to save money. We opened our first office space in a small loft in an industrial warehouse. With the help of my friend Patrick Stycos, we built an apartment inside this loft, and built a smaller apartment inside this apartment so Morgan and I could live, eat, and sleep Blavity."

—AARON SAMUELS, COFOUNDER OF
BLAVITY (POSTING ON LINKEDIN)

You've got to watch the numbers and manage and monitor your burn, which I cover in the next chapter. You must monitor your expenses on a regular basis. You should look at the financials at least weekly or biweekly. In those early days, the seed money is your lifeblood pumping through the veins, especially if you don't have money coming back in.

You've got to get laser-focused on what you're doing, where you're spending this money and why, and your desired result. You have six months to take the seed money and show that forward momentum, show something good is coming out of the investment, that you're making waves in the industry, gaining customers, and building on your prototype. No one's going to give you more money if you're not showing progress and if you're not achieving traction. You want to prove your product is viable in the marketplace to attract the investors for the second round.

"It's okay to not have it all figured out! Like most entrepreneurs who are just getting started, there was no playbook for what we were building at Away, so we were figuring out everything ourselves for the first time and learning every single day. You're bound to make a few mistakes, but that creates a ton of learning opportunities, and mistakes also mean that you're being bold with your ideas and taking risks—which will ultimately move your business forward more meaningfully than if you're too afraid to take any risks."

—JEN RUBIO, COFOUNDER AND CHIEF
BRAND OFFICER OF AWAY

BUILD YOUR TEAM

We were experienced businesswomen by the time we received the first round of funding. We already had a product that clients were using, so we focused on building our team, starting to hire key staff members, and paying ourselves a reasonable salary. As clients began using our product more, there were fees that we incurred, such as hosting and pipeline fees.

I have seen other startups wobble at this point, particularly when they're founded by people who are slanted in one direction; for example, the founders are more comfortable with engineering or marketing, and they build a team of all engineers or all marketers. New founders risk focusing so much on developing the product or getting clients that they neglect the fact that the business is, in part, built on revenue and reputation.

Sometimes it gets ugly. I witnessed a situation in which the visionary had an incredible understanding of the audience for their product but had less business acumen than his operations partner. The COO wanted to control everything and took advantage of the visionary's lack of business savvy. He gradually took away the visionary's control and input to making decisions, eventually edging him out completely. This led to the death of the company through shortsighted power dynamics. Happens all the time in various ways.

You have to have those four key team members we talked about in Chapter 3. To build that well-rounded team, you don't want to overspend on one area to the exclusion of other areas just because that's the area you know and are comfortable with. It's great if you're an intense marketer and you can jam on marketing, but that's not going to help you if you don't actually have a product to sell.

You can't just rely on sales. You have to back that up with an actual, a solid product or service. I've also seen start-ups who are selling vaporware. These founders have a product that both gives you the vapors, because it sounds cool, but also evaporates, because there is no actual product. These are products a customer will purchase and then find out they don't work. We had a competitor in our marketplace early on who was selling a similar-sounding product, but we heard from clients and customers that once they tried it, there was no there, there. It didn't actually work. The product was buggy and nonfunctional.

DAY-TO-DAY OPERATIONS

Closely examining each expenditure and decision helps you spend efficiently and see opportunities. When you look at expenditures, you're looking at the numbers, but perhaps more importantly, you're looking at the results those expenditures bring. You've got to figure out what actions are most successful in generating leads.

As a founder, your job, ultimately, is to oversee everything, but that doesn't mean you should be trying to do everything. You have a team, and you need to assign roles. It's incumbent upon you to look at the numbers, to ask questions, to observe results, and to make decisions accordingly, as quickly as possible.

You don't want to be a micromanager, particularly in a startup. Your team needs to function well as a cohesive unit. However, there are certain principles that, hopefully, you are inculcating with your team. You want to have three big, important KPIs (key performance indicators) that you're tracking. You should be working with each of your team members to make sure that they have three KPIs that they are focused on.

As a manager, it's not humanly possible for you to make every single decision. You'll make big decisions with your co-founders or core team members. When we had a big decision to make about funding or the direction of the business, Roz and I would talk about it. Day-to-day decisions were made by Roz with Cindy, our CTO, and the rest of the team. Team members make decisions every day on their own with some initial and continuing guidance from the management team.

PAY YOUR TAXES

It's already stressful having a startup. You don't want to add more stress by screwing up on just the basics of running your business and taking care of your employees. You need someone to manage the books, and whoever is managing your books, invoicing, accounts payable, can also manage the PEO relationship. Someone has to be in charge of that stuff because it doesn't happen on its own. Those W-2s and W-4s aren't just going to magically fill themselves out. Workers comp—somebody's got to fill out those forms.

You need to pay your taxes, your personal and your business taxes. Make sure you're filing everyone's I-9s and W-2s. It seems like a small thing, but forgetting to pay attention to the tax law and to pay those tax bills can damage your business, your reputation, and your revenue if you end up having to pay penalties, fines, and attorneys. Keep in mind that corporate taxes have different deadlines than your personal taxes. Professional employer organizations (PEOs) like Insperity, Zenefits, or TriNet can think about taxes and payroll and human resources for you. It can at least seem pricey at first, but it's far pricier if you have to pay fines and attorneys. It's worth the money to stay out of trouble and make sure your business and employees are taken care of, so you can focus your attention and your money on other matters.

HIRE SLOW, FIRE FAST

Everybody on your team is going to be pretty busy that first year. Sometimes, within the first year or two, it's clear that there is a person who's not able to scale with the business. The stress gets to people and changes them. I gained a lot of weight in the startup years. I was able to lose it later, but the level of stress and responsibility puts a strain on your relationships, your personality, and your sanity. The stress can bring out some unfortunate characteristics that you may have glimpsed before but are now in full turkey display. If someone is starting to wander into territory that is not helpful for them, the business, or both, it's better to have an initial conversation and see if that helps. Make a decision within a quarter if someone is just not able to move forward and grow with the business.

Don't keep someone on staff if it's not the right fit. We had to let our initial CMO go within three months of him being with us. That was a tough decision. He was a major hire, but it was clear early on that he wasn't the right fit. His salary was burning up a bunch of our seed capital, so he had to go.

Don't be afraid to let nonproducers go. Likewise, don't be afraid to move people around to different roles. If it's clear someone is a better fit in a different role, change it up. Everyone's going to be wearing a lot of different hats in the early startup days; you may hire someone to do one thing, but in fact, they're great at another thing. Move them if they're delivering. Lean into that, pivot, and figure out how to fill that original role some other way.

ROZ TALKS ABOUT SCALING

In the beginning, one sales lead and I were selling the product. He was able to sell thirty-thousand dollars' worth of our product a month, so my thinking was, *If we had five sales guys, we'd sell $150,000 a month.* The assumption of linear growth with additional sales people is a mistake I see entrepreneurs make all the time. We hired additional sales people too soon and didn't invest enough in early product discovery and iteration.

After you've had some sales, it's tempting to say to investors: "We've got the product. It's selling. Now we just need more sales people, so we can sell more." The problem is that if you've only sold to early adopters, you likely don't yet have a product that will cross the chasm and appeal to the more conservative middle-market buyer, i.e., you don't *really* have a market-ready product. If you've told investors you're using their money to scale sales, you may end up with a bunch of sales onpeople who can't close deals and with too slim a product team to meet the needs of the market they're trying to address.

Business-to-business sales is tough because it can take months to close a sale. For example, for us, our sales person took three to six months to lock down a new customer. We had one sales person, and we hired three more the day we closed our second round of funding. We blew through a lot of our larger second round trying to ramp up sales, waiting six months while paying three people full time before we realized they couldn't do it. That was a painful lesson.

Roles often change as you scale your company. I've seen a situation with a tech startup recently in which someone who was extremely important at the founding stage turned out to be a terrible manager, and that company let the person go. The longer you wait, hoping that person will change, grow up, or evolve, the bigger the impact on your company and your team. Again, sometimes those people have to be let go, and those are hard but important decisions to make, especially when the person who was an integral part of your initial success has become a liability to your future success.

The decision becomes complicated when the nonperformers have equity and you have to negotiate losing some of the equity that would go to a new person you hire for that position. For example, your CTO may be a great technologist but doesn't have a clue how to manage developers. Talk with the person frankly about the problem and look for ways to maneuver them into a productive role, knowing they can't keep the CTO title in name only. This problem of growth and scale happens all the time in startups, tech and nontech. Elon Musk has publicly recounted his personal and professional challenges as his businesses have grown. All the more reason to choose your partners and early team members with an eye to the future.

Be honest about your own skills. Sometimes, the problem

is you. You may reach a point and realize you were a great founder with a small team, but you don't have the skill to grow your company. You don't want to see your struggle and hard work implode because of your ego. Hire a COO who can take the reins to grow your company.

SHARE THE VISION

Lack of a shared vision commonly causes the downfall of a fledgling startup. Sometimes it's an ego problem. Sometimes one person isn't pulling their weight. For example, if one or two people are doing 80 percent of the work, and the other people are doing 20 percent but everyone has equal equity, that's a situation that creates real tension. On the one hand, if someone is working 20 percent of their time but bringing in 80 percent of the business, that's a good deal for everyone. On the other hand, if someone is working 20 percent of the time and bringing in 10 percent of the business, something has to change and, more than likely, that person has to go.

At some point in your startup, you'll need to pivot. As you road test your product and gather new information about what your target audience needs and how customers use your product, you'll have to shift gears to keep the company alive. At that moment, there's often one founder who understands the pivot and moves guns-a-blazing in that direction, and there's another founder who's stuck in the original vision who can't evolve with the new information. As a company, you have to address this challenge as quickly as possible, which might mean moving someone off your team. It always comes down to people.

MAKE QUICK DECISIONS

You have to make a lot of decisions in those first six months, and every decision impacts burn. You have to allocate your resources and divide them between your user experience, the dissection of the product, your backend, sales materials, and marketing. The faster you can look at the results of your decisions and then make another decision, the better you'll manage that burn. People tend to spend unwisely because they're not keeping their eye on the ball. You have to be ruthless and vigorous about whether you're getting results from a person or a program, your PR agency. Every choice has an impact.

Don't give your decisions more than sixty to ninety days to show results. If you're not getting traction, pivot. Make a different decision. The situation will not look better after another sixty to ninety days. With our CMO, we knew within the first month that it wasn't going to work out. It took us another couple of months to decide to let him go because we were paying that dude a lot of money and really needed a marketing expert. Keeping him longer than we should have delayed finding a different talented marketing person who would have been a better fit.

Those delayed decisions have a ripple effect. We'd already lost money and time on that person. We also lost money and time and were delayed in achieving the results that we were trying to get.

"I would have started sooner with everything. I also would have stuck up for myself more. I would have done the hardest things, because eventually you will have to, and most of all, I would have trusted my gut a lot more in terms of the wrong hires, wrong advisors, etc., etc. I would have tried to make revenue quicker, because we could have if I would have just believed in myself and my capabilities."
—ASHLEY M. WILLAMS, FOUNDER AND CEO OF RIZZARR

Sometimes delayed decisions equal missed opportunities. Once we had a great marketing person, Jeanette Russell, we put together a guide about using the product that was, by default, a guide about influencer engagement. The guide was hugely popular and a great source of leads, but six months passed before we saw it as a lead generator and thought of creating more guides. We dragged our feet unnecessarily on that opportunity.

SPEEDBUMP

Chances are, you've been undercapitalized. You probably don't have as much money to play with as your white male Silicon Valley friends. Your runway is shorter, and it will take you longer to raise the next round. This is not the time to buy a new house with somebody else's money. Until you go through another round of funding or bring on customers, you're not going to get more money. Bottom line, if you misspend that seed capital, the longevity of your business will be short.

INVESTOR EYE-OPENER

The seed round up to Series A isn't the time to cheap out. Female and minority founders tend to be undercapitalized. If you're serious about investing in and creating this new economy with founders who are bringing new ideas, products, and services to the table, you have to invest enough, so there's a real chance for success. Because they are nontraditional founders, they might actually need a little more than you would normally invest.

Research published by the Boston Consulting Group[15] shows that female entrepreneurs generate revenue more quickly than men. They write, "The average startup that

---

15   Katie Abouzahr, Frances Brooks Taplett, Matt Krentz, John Harthorne, "Why Women-Owned Startups Are a Better Bet," *Boston Consulting Group*, June 6, 2018. https://www.bcg.com/publications/2018/why-women-owned-startups-are-better-bet.aspx

had been founded or co-founded by women received $935,000, or less than half the $2.12 million that the male-founded companies had received. Despite that funding gap, the women-owned companies had generated more in revenue over a five-year period: $730,000 compared with $662,000. For every dollar of funding, the women-owned startups had generated seventy-eight cents in revenue, while those founded by men had generated less than half that amount—just thirty-one cents. In this sample, if investors had put the same amount of capital into the startups that were founded or co-founded by women as they had into those founded by men, an additional eighty-five million dollars would have been generated over the five-year period studied."

CHAPTER 7

TRACTION AND BURN

We raised our second round of funding, Series A, on the strength of our belief that we could expand the appeal of Attentive.ly to the private sector. Our product had been inspired by products that were in the for-profit sector, and the idea was to bring some of that technology and customize it for nonprofits and their specific needs. Our product was as good or better than what some companies were using. We asked ourselves if there was a bigger potential market that could take our business to a different level.

SPEND MONEY TO MAKE MONEY

A natural tension occurs between traction and burn. You want to spend, or burn, your money in such a way that you're achieving significant traction, either in an increase in sales or monthly users, however you measure your traction. The ideal scenario is your traction is greater than your burn. Remember, your runway, or financial resources, is shorter than you think.

The other end of the spectrum is a startup's nightmare. If you have high burn and low traction, if you're spending a lot of money with zero or negative results, you will rapidly find yourself out of business. Low traction and high burn is a clear indication that you're not good at this. You should stop what you're doing, take a step back, and get help to figure out what you're doing wrong.

Most businesses fail in the first year. Of those that survive, most fail in their third year. We were in our third year and rolling along. After the second funding round, we had a sales person dedicated to business-oriented companies instead of nonprofits. Because we'd had success, we thought we could gain traction in the private sector. We were encouraged when we signed a Fortune 10 client, but when we looked at the numbers, the effort didn't pay off for us. Our sales cycle was normally sixty to ninety days; however, large organizations tend to move more slowly, so getting to that number took a little longer. We tried hard, giving it close to a year to take off. We were concerned about letting down investors who believed in us, but we had to be honest with ourselves and our investors and admit that our efforts to enter the private market weren't working.

When you're having trouble gaining traction with customers, rarely is there one issue. It's often an unfortunate combination of factors, and you need to analyze the interactions and think about how you can twiddle the knobs a bit or make a big shift in a different direction that's going to make more sense for everybody.

In our case, the combination was more competition, more products available for the for-profit sector, and customers who were happily using something else and didn't see a reason to change even if our product was better. The for-profit sector was definitely more mature in its use of tools like Attentive.ly. The language we used to describe Attentive.ly was geared for nonprofits. Even though the activities were similar, the way that nonprofits describe those activities is different, and even the goal can be different than corporate goals. Shifting gears was difficult for our sales team because we didn't have the materials or lingo that appealed to the for-profit sector.

You can always "give it more time," but every day that you spend working on something that doesn't work means that you're accelerating your burn and making it more of a challenge to stay alive when things get tough or when the well starts to run dry. The dream for most startups is to go big.

Any moment that you're spending money and time doing

something that's not working means that you're not doing something that might work. It's fairly binary that way. There's always a trade-off. Whether you're going for a little higher risk and, therefore, a little higher reward or you're trying to steer the rudder, keep the rudder steady and make what might seem like incremental progress. Of course, investors, all investors, are hoping for the moon shot where there's kind of a big blowout. It's a delicate balance between those two.

The challenge for any company is to make decisions that balance investing in existing markets and breaking into new ones. If you're successful in your core market, it can make more sense to look for ways to expand that core market rather than break into new markets. For us, when we realized we weren't gaining the traction we needed from the private sector, we stepped back and expanded in the nonprofit sector where we already had traction.

ROZ TALKS ABOUT SALES

How you'll sell your product depends on what you're selling. If your product is anything under twelve hundred dollars a year, the validation is through self-serve sales. A small investment in ads and a self-serve workflow works. You need to keep working on the product until it literally sells itself; otherwise, that business strategy won't work. If it's higher dollar sales, you have even more risk because you can actually generate a fair bit of revenue up front. The chart below shows the curve of early adopters, then there's a gap before you have the bulk of average customers and then laggards. Don't be fooled by those early adopters and B2B sales, where you have higher-dollar sales. Be aware of this curve and plan for it.

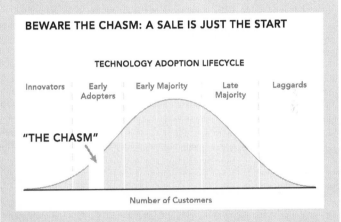

BEWARE THE CHASM: A SALE IS JUST THE START

TECHNOLOGY ADOPTION LIFECYCLE

If you've got a new technology, assume those first one hundred sales are early adopters. Don't assume you'll have linear growth from there. Utilize the dollars coming in to improve your product, not scale sales. It's tempting to demonstrate those first sales to investors to get more funding, but if you haven't yet hit that gap between early adopters and the average customer, then you should still be in product-validation mode, and all of those dollars should be going back into the designing, measuring, and iterating, not throwing more sales people at it.

It's better to take it slow up front. Raise more capital or find ways to do it on the cheap, and perfect the product rather than race so quickly to revenues. Take the time to do true market validation, get the product to the point where it can be sold by Joe Schmo down the street or it can sell without a sales person. Only when you can hand it to a sales person, and they can sell a million dollars' worth of your product, have you truly validated your idea.

If your traction isn't defined as sales, make sure you've got something to show for it. For example, the traction for Facebook or Twitter when they started wasn't sales; it was sheer audience and base. If you've got a burn going on, there should be something pretty dramatic on the other end that looks like traction, either in terms of users and customers, sales, or ideally both.

We live in a volatile environment today. You may have a reasonable ratio between burn and traction, and all of a sudden, something changes. For example, Twitter purchased one of the vendors for our information feed, and suddenly, the price for providing our product increased on the backend, and we had to shift our pricing model accordingly to keep up. You have to keep an eye out for those types of changes.

When you have good traction, you hire more people to maintain it, and depending on how well the staff is performing, your burn can start to increase. The ratio of burn to traction changes because you have more people. Those people have to be trained before they're producing. You have to keep a constant eye on the traction, the rate at which you're bringing in business, versus where the money is going and how fast it's going out. You have to be in a position to spot changes in the environment and in your company and make appropriate decisions to stay on track.

If your burn is high because of low sales, look at your pricing model and structure. Pricing is a big deal for startups, not just the amount but also how to structure the pricing. For example, does a monthly or annual subscription model make the most sense for your customer? Consider experimenting to see if restructuring pricing makes a sale more of a slam dunk for customers. We worked hard on pricing in the nonprofit sector. We started off with a monthly payment and then moved to an annual payment because it was better for our cash flow and, surprisingly, an easier sale.

WHAT I WOULD DO DIFFERENTLY

Looking back, I wish we had been more structured in our efforts to enter a new market. We should have had a clearer sense of what we were testing and how we would know our efforts were working. If I were doing it today, I would also set a time limit for deciding when we needed to move forward or when we needed to pivot and cut our losses. I would have made the decision sooner to cut certain efforts. There were decisions we could have made at the three-month mark after having gone through the first sales cycle where we still waited for more evidence to build, for example.

Our efforts to break into the private sector set us back. We used up a lot of our runway when we weren't pulling in customers. Roz and I talked about it. We discussed shifting our focus back to nonprofits with our board of directors, which included two investors from Atlanta Technology Angels, Roz, and me. We listened to their input and got them on board, giving us a united front when we reported the shift back to our investors. Our Series A investors were interested in the private sector, but ultimately, they wanted us to have a viable, successful business that was headed toward break-even and profitability.

"You (the founder) have to set goals and be accountable for them. HOWEVER, you don't have to meet those goals; in fact, those goals can (and probably should) change over time as you learn more about your market, customer, competition, and yourself/team (i.e., what are you all good at? What's working?). You just need to communicate enough with your investors/stakeholders such that they understand why the

first set of goals haven't been reached, what you learned from that, and why the next set of goals make more sense for your growth. Each founder's grasp and facility with this loop is a key area of assessment for me."

—JOSEPH THURAKAL, SENIOR PORTFOLIO MANAGER
OF TIGMERA (AN ANGEL IMPACT INVESTMENT FUND)

If you're seeking to expand into new markets, that's great. You should definitely give it a try, but don't be overconfident. Do your homework. Make sure you're speaking the language of this new audience. Make sure that you have customized materials for that audience. Figure out their likes and dislikes, what's working, and what's not. Give it a time period. If we're not able to sell X number of licenses or widgets within X period of time, let's pull out so that we can make sure that we're managing our burn. In short, if you're not receiving traction within a given amount of time, you're just accelerating the burn.

DAY-TO-DAY TRACKING

Every startup is a little different. Traction or burn might look different if you're manufacturing a physical product as opposed to a social network, or as opposed to software as a service. Your balance of traction to burn depends on your product. You're the one who has to look at your accounting numbers and make sure you can tell not just a fantasy story, not just a story that's going to keep your investors and your staff reasonably calm, but a story that you believe, that you actually feel good about.

The mistake a lot of inexperienced startup founders make is not having a methodical approach. Your startup was born out of and empowered by hope. You've got to keep that hope and optimism and confidence there because your hope will buoy you, but below that buoy, you need some kind of weight that's going to hold you so that the buoy doesn't float off into the ocean. The weight—the methodical approach—keeps the buoy in place and keeps it stable so that it continues to provide that signal. The hope is that signal point floating above all of the churn.

The spreadsheets and balance sheets are the weight. Take an honest, daily look at your progress, your accounts payable, accounts receivable, sales numbers, and customer feedback. All of that data ultimately is the weight that's going to keep your business grounded and stable.

If the burn is going too quickly, if resources are moving out without a lot of return, you've got to slow down. Take a deep breath and look at your numbers. You should have the data in front of you or should be able to pull it. Find the leaky pipe and plug it. Look where the money's going and look for some other place to put your money that's showing promise. Identify the activities that are generating leads and closing sales and the activities that aren't.

Stop doing the things that aren't working and lean in to the things that are working.

It may sound simple. It's not. It's a lot of work and emotional labor to be honest with yourself about the things that aren't working, because sometimes those things are people. Sometimes it's a person that just isn't the right fit or isn't capable of doing the job that you need. Sometimes the leaky pipe is a person who has to leave, so you can reallocate those resources to a different type of staffer.

That's a tough decision to make, but it's the decision that you should make within sixty to ninety days. In a startup, no person is indispensable. You have to be looking at the performance of every person weekly. Every person's effort has to add up to something; otherwise, they are generating burn and not traction.

STRATEGIC BURN

You want to invest in yourself. Your investors have invested in you, and you need to do the same. When we started, it was clear from working with our customer success team that our customers loved the concept of Attentive.ly, but they weren't ultimately sure what to do once they were in there. Attentive.ly provided a sophisticated tool set, but the techniques to use the tool set were unique as well.

With that information, we invested in ways to provide recommendations, wizards, that pulled up encouraging data and gave a suggestion of how to use it. For example, a user might receive a message that said, "Here are the top ten people talking about you today. Here are the top ten hashtags. Do you want to use one of these?" We invested in making the user interface easier to use and that ended up being a good choice, but it definitely created a certain amount of burn to build out the feature set of the product rather than just hoping our customers would figure it out. It was clear that they wouldn't.

Another strategic use of burn was giving away a free match to generate leads. In exchange for five thousand email addresses, we offered potential customers a complimentary look at a set of five thousand random people to show them what it looked like in social media. It wasn't the full dashboard, but rather an abbreviated PDF version so they could understand what they'd find in our product. Building that out took energy at first, and we saw good results from it.

And that's the whole point. It's okay, important even, to spend and invest in certain areas. You need to keep an eye on the results of the investment. If you get something from it, build on and do more of it. If you don't get anything from it, pivot in another direction.

We invested in marketing that gave potential customers a

taste of our product. We had cards printed with a special URL where people could go and get some kind of freebie. We offered the free match, the report, and the guides mentioned in Chapter 6.

Not all of our investments paid off. We spent money trying to make the product more self-service. Our dream was that people could simply buy the product without us having to do anything. Put their credit card number in and go to town. Who wouldn't want that? The whole passive income market is built on that. It didn't work for our audience. It was a major purchase for our customers, and they needed help with onboarding and training. The money we invested in a do-it-yourself version didn't come back.

DON'T WORRY ABOUT THE JONESES

Focus your attention on having the best possible product or service. Environmental awareness is important, but being obsessed with your competition only serves to drain energy from being focused on your own external and internal imperatives that keep the business alive and growing.

You can't measure yourself simply by comparing your revenue or company size to someone else in your sector. You have to look at the quality of your product or service too. Another company may be larger than yours, but you may be doing the same thing better. It's common to see acquisitions take place because the startup has more sophisticated technology. It's easier and often preferable for them to purchase the more sophisticated technology if they can do a better job selling it because they already have the market.

Ultimately, focus on building a good and viable business as opposed to keeping up with the Joneses. I've seen founders spend too much time looking outward instead of looking at their business, their startup, and figuring out how to make it the best startup possible with the best culture and the best people.

Potential acquirers watch to see which startups are growing faster, achieving greater market share, or producing a better product. They'll know about your competition better than you do. Gauge your position in the market by talking with your strategic partners and potential acquirers, with whom you should be building a relationship as you see your business taking off and as you prepare to exit.

SPEEDBUMP

You have to manage your burn carefully so that you don't run out of steam. Be careful, and be smart about stretching that dollar as far as you can. Because you are a nontraditional founder, you will be under more scrutiny than a traditional founder. Your investors are going to be watching more carefully, even if they believe in you and are neither sexist nor racist. It's just a question of implicit or hidden bias. Stay on the up and up. Don't fudge the numbers on your financial disclosures or profit and loss statements. Don't try to hide money you spent on one thing by putting it in a different category. Be transparent and clear about your rate of traction and burn.

INVESTOR EYE-OPENER

The best investors ask questions. Offer help if you can see that the numbers aren't quite adding up or you want more numbers. Keep your questions friendly because you don't want to put the founder on the defensive, and you don't want to interfere or seem to be intervening in too muscular a way. Be proactive in offering help because a nontraditional founder might feel less confidence in coming to you for support. It doesn't mean they don't want support or don't respect you, but don't assume they have the same level of confidence that a white guy would have to ask for help or for more funding.

CHAPTER 8

EXIT STRATEGY

At some point, you have to decide whether or not it's time to exit. If you're smart, you should have an exit strategy from the beginning. Knowing what you want your exit to look like means you maintain control over how you exit; otherwise, the exit will happen to you. Your exit may be imminent in your future, and you don't even realize it. That certainly happened to us.

Being acquired was our exit strategy from the beginning. We knew our business would not reach a size to instigate an IPO, and we were fine with that. We knew it was likely that someone would want to bring our technology in-house. Most of the big businesses decide whether or not to acquire along a few different lines, but the essential decision hinges around whether it's easier to build new technology or buy it. Large organizations tend to move slowly, and it's challenging to stimulate a hothouse of innovation at a certain level of size and maturity. That's why acquisitions happen. They say, "Wow. That's there. It's ready to go. All we need to do is take it."

We were persuasive with acquirers in demonstrating there was no way that they were going to build Attentive. ly. We'd done a lot of research and had all the reasons why it made sense for a company to acquire us. We had strong relationships with the social media platforms. We'd developed a great user interface that'd been tested. A company would spend a lot more money trying to emulate what we've done without having the same success or whitelisting on certain platforms.

Attentive.ly and Blackbaud had a solid existing relationship, and we were card-carrying members in the Blackbaud Partner Program. They liked us. We had a good reputation. We shared clients, so clients that they wanted to keep or that they wanted to build upon were using our platform. They readily saw they could add their sales team and their contacts and expand the Attentive. ly sales process quite dramatically. They weren't going to have to spend millions of dollars over three to five years trying to build the same tool. We offered plug and play, and that's why acquisitions happen.

THINK ABOUT LEAVING WHEN YOU LAUNCH

Think about your exit strategy as soon as you begin to look for funding because your investors will want to know your plan. They want to understand you have a strong sense of your business life cycle and the potential endgame because they're investing with the endgame in mind. Your investors don't want to lose money, but they understand they're placing bets. They know most will be losing bets, and a couple will be big winners. They spread their risk across multiple investments, and when they hit a supernova or unicorn, the risks become worthwhile.

Tricia Salinero, who is the managing director at Woodside Capital Partners and the rare senior merger and acquisitions (M&A) exec who is a woman, took Attentive.ly on as a client even though she normally works on much bigger projects. She and other M&A folks we interviewed told us we were the kind of startup they originally got into the business to help. She was an amazing guide through the labyrinth that is the M&A journey. I asked her, "What's the one thing you wish every entrepreneur knew that would make all the difference during the M&A process?" and she said,

> Always: Anecdotally, 75 percent of the time, you will be bought by a company that "meets" you as a customer or as a competitor. Be noisy. Talk to analysts, influencers, and publishers to make your case. Keep your website up to date

and put out press releases (even if only on your website, which is free) on a consistent basis. Develop friends and alliances in the market. Make it easy to be found.

Before the deal: Understand the difference between cash versus accrual accounting. CEOs *buy* on strategy, but CFOs *pay* on GAAP accounting, and untangling those differences can sometimes create a delta in perceived value for the buyer and seller.

During the deal: Make your projections—it builds trust with the buyer. The number one deal killer is missing the forecast during the process. Taking your eyes off the prize— your company—to fill one more due diligence request will ultimately hurt the deal. Missing the numbers by a LOT suggests that you don't understand the pipeline and conversion rates in your own business.

Overall: There are three thousand to five thousand tech deals a year. The most active buyer might do twenty deals in a year, which means that there is a loooooong tail of acquirers. Look beyond the Googles, Facebooks, Apples, and Microsofts of the world.

As you think about your exit strategy, consider the likely life cycle for your type of product. Looking into the future changes how you see your strategic partners, who could become acquirers. Acquisitions often spring from good, long-term relationships. The people who are most familiar with your product appreciate its usefulness and begin to see opportunities for how they could benefit if your product were part of their wheelhouse.

> ## ROZ TALKS ABOUT DOING THE MATH
>
> You have to do the math at the beginning to build a business that is big and compelling enough for someone to want to buy it if your endgame is to sell the business. Most entrepreneurs start a product business with the thought, *I wish I had this thing.* They don't understand that there must be enough customers with the same pain point who are willing to pay for the product such that there is a sales strategy that maps to scaling the business.

THREE-WAY EXIT

There are three ways to exit. There is an IPO, which happens for only a small fraction of startups. There is being acquired, which is the most likely route if you're successful. Third, because 80 to 90 percent of startups fail, you're just going to go out of business. You'll have to close up and move on. There's talk about alternative exits, but most of the alternative exits that I've seen don't look like exiting, they look like continuing to have a business, which isn't an exit to me.

That said, in Chapter Four, I mentioned the concept of steward ownership, which is becoming popular in Europe and getting introduced to the American startup scene. It's a scenario in which an investor understands that the business has a social mission and has specifically negotiated not for future speculative "hockey stick"–style huge returns on investment (ROI), but on capped dividends (sometimes called demand dividends).

As Max Slavkin of Creative Action Network wrote on *Medium*,

> Once we hit a certain revenue threshold, we start paying a portion of our profits back to our investors, until they've all received five times their initial investment. That solved the "exit" problem and meant investors can make a solid return without CAN ever being sold. Finally, we'd found a way to raise money that actually reflected our goals and our values.

BE TECHNOLOGICALLY COMPATIBLE

Right from the beginning, you probably have some ideas about who would be a potential acquirer. Keep those companies in mind as you build out the technology of your product and build in compatibility for APIs that align with your strategic partners and acquirers. If you think LinkedIn would be a good acquirer in the future, make sure you are innovating with the LinkedIn APIs. If you're hoping

Apple will buy you, make sure you're deeply embedded in the Apple SDK, their developer kit. Potential acquirers will want to see compatibility.

We had strategic partnerships with customer relationship management software companies (CRMs) in our space, and we made sure to use the API from their tools to make it easy for customers to move data back and forth between Attentive.ly and their CRM. We did that with a lot of CRMs, and it was beneficial for both sides. The CRMs could offer additional, next-generation functionality to their clients. We were able to do joint marketing and sales at times. This was great in the moment and for the future because we got to know each other and see how well our software worked with their software.

LISTEN FOR CODE WORDS

There are code words. When a strategic partner takes you to lunch and says they want to "deepen the relationship," chances are they are testing the waters for acquiring your company. If, on the other hand, they want to "strengthen the relationship," they're interested in doing things together and being generally supportive. A deeper relationship means they want to business-marry you.

With Attentive.ly, we reached a point where it was clear by looking at the numbers that we were going to need to do another round. We had to choose between another Series A round, a larger Series B round, or approaching people to whom we could sell. We took the lead on approaching companies. We approached companies that we knew and had strong relationships with and some that we didn't know but who were aware of us. Sometimes you will be approached, which happened to one startup I know. They were approached by one of the big five tech companies early in their startup journey and weren't ready.

It can be heady when a big company like Facebook, Amazon, or Microsoft wants to deepen the relationship with you. After living the intensity of launching a startup, it can be hard to imagine what your life will look like postmerger. All the more reason to have thought about your exit strategy from the beginning. The first time they were approached, this startup was still building the business. It's a big change to go from running your own shop, making all the decisions, and managing a small, energized team to being swallowed by a larger, established organization and having to work within their culture. The second time Facebook approached them, they were ready to have that conversation.

INFLECTION POINTS

If you're still in the game legitimately after a year or eighteen months and you've got something to show for that time frame, pop the champagne cork. You've already cleared the first hurdle.

The next hurdle is the three-year mark. At the three-year mark, you might be tired. You've been working hard, and it's natural to want to take a deep breath and hope that things are on the rails, but nothing is on the rails. Your train could derail at any minute, and you need to continue to act like it all the way through the third year.

Many startups, and businesses in general, will fail at this point. You risk falling prey to complacency, especially if things are going well. You've established a rhythm, yet it's important to stay hungry and not lose ground. When you start to get comfortable, you're likely to miss something or not make that decision that needs to be made quickly enough and then pay for your lax behavior later.

Clients have a habit of wandering off around the three-year mark. You have to innovate because customers want the next new thing. Every day, your customers could decide to try something new simply because it's new, even though that new, hot product might be inferior to yours. It's frustrating when people leave you for an inferior product that has great sales patois. There's always competition. Make sure that you aren't overly confident about your current customer base and continue to work hard to broaden your sales.

If you can clear the three-year mark and maintain the business momentum as well as your own mental and emotional momentum, you have a good chance of reaching the next inflection point.

If your company is red hot, acquirers may come knocking at your door in the three-to-five-year phase, and you have to decide if it's the right time to be acquired or if you feel there's more you want or can do with the product.

ROZ TALKS ABOUT SUBSEQUENT FUNDING ROUNDS

It took us that twelve months to raise our first $375,000. By the last set of rounds, we raised $1.5 million in about nine months. If the business is still growing, existing investors will reinvest. They tend to reinvest pro rata, so you get a baseline of cash coming in with each new round. It's easier to find someone to lead a round. You find more institutional investors whose profile you fit. The name of your company is out there, and you're able to better articulate what you do. As long as the business continues to grow, the fundraising picks up speed and size.

THE FIVE-YEAR MARK

For a startup, five to seven years can sound old. Certainly

you may feel much older if you've gotten this far! If you continue to innovate, you won't be seen as old but rather as the standard for how people do what you do. You will have created a new best practice or best product. At that point, you're a leader among peers. By five to seven years, you're no longer an experiment and usually stable enough to be interesting to acquirers. You've built a strong reputation by now, and you have the relationships wherein that acquisition starts to make a lot of sense. You're not a cute, fleeting idea anymore. You have the maturity for people to see the staying power of your technology and the need to incorporate it into their own product line.

If you've reached the five-to-seven-year mark, and you're not thinking about your exit strategy, it's time. At that point you're often faced with a decision: raise another round of funding or sell your company. If an IPO is your exit strategy, then you're going to deepen your relationship with the Securities and Exchange Commission. Again, IPOs are a fraction of the existing tech companies. Either option takes about the same amount of time, six to twelve months. Look around to see if other people in your space, including your competitors, are getting acquired.

LOOK FOR ACQUIRERS

You can go for a long time as a startup and not make enough money. You might be making money and building the business but not breaking even, let alone making a profit. Many startups, even famous ones like Facebook, Twitter, and Google, were considered successful yet weren't profitable for a long time. That's why there are Series D funding rounds. You may reach a certain break-even level and see another goalpost that would allow you to be a bigger company, but you have to spend money to make money. Again, this is where burn and traction come into play. Facebook and Twitter had amazing traction and influence, but they had to figure out how to make money from what they were doing. Google had a similar experience. Tesla still isn't making money.

You can be considered an extremely successful business and continue to raise money on the future promise of making a ton of cash. Moore's Law can play into it in terms of the time it takes for the business to hit. Investors are looking for some evidence that there's a viable business in the future. You want to demonstrate a strong trajectory of people either using and/or buying the product.

You don't want just anyone to acquire you, and you don't want to reach a point of desperation because that tends to lead to bad money or a bad deal. It's a two-way street. If being acquired is your exit strategy, planning ahead gives you more control over the negotiations and who acquires you. You want to be acquired by a company that feels like a good fit, not by someone who's going to come in, dump your team, and take the technology. You may have spent close to a decade thinking about and building your product, but only so many people will appreciate its genius. Likewise, only so many people that you want to be acquired by will have the means to do so. It's a little like musical chairs, and you don't want to be one of two people fighting over the last chair.

WHAT ACQUIRERS LOOK FOR IN YOU

While you are looking for acquirers, large companies have staff dedicated to looking for companies like yours to acquire. It can help to get inside their heads so you're better prepared to position your company as you begin the dance of conversation about "deepening your relationship." Tech companies need to stay on the cutting edge, and new products are the name of the game. They continually consider whether it's a better business decision to build that new product or acquire a company that's already making a product that fits with their suite.

Kevin McDearis is the EVP and Chief Products Officer at Blackbaud, which acquired Roz's and my company Attentive.ly. His input is essential in the process of deciding whether or not Blackbaud will build or buy new tech. I asked him what he looks for when he considers acquiring a company. He gave me his criteria rundown:

1. Market opportunity: is the payback big enough to justify the expense? Payback may be something more than just revenue or profit. It could include things like technology advance, market share, or customer retention.
2. Cultural fit, talent, skill, and experience of the team: in nine out of ten M&As, the acquisition is about the IP contained in the people. Know who they are, how they will or won't fit, and if they will want to stay or go.
3. Technology leverage: is it a fit, a fix, or an outright rebuild? There's justification for any scenario, but you need to understand the scenario to truly gauge #1.
4. Operating leverage: how well is the company run from an HR and finance standpoint? Is the accounting sound? Are there hidden legal or financial risks? How much can be saved or reinvested if duplicate functions are appropriately optimized?

CHOOSING AN M&A CHAMPION

Don't try to sell your company by yourself. Merging with or being acquired by a larger company is not for the faint at heart. You need a mergers and acquisitions (M&A) specialist, like Tricia, who will champion and represent you to potential acquirers. You need someone who understands the market, has a good reputation in their field, and has expertise and relationships. Your M&A champion will approach acquirers and, eventually, negotiate the sale.

More importantly, you need someone who gets you, empathizes with you, and can get inside your head to make the right call when you aren't present. This person will be *you* in meetings with potential acquirers and must represent your best interest in those meetings, where you will not be present. You have to be able to trust this person 100 percent.

For us, it was a challenge to find someone who had experience representing women and minority startup owners. We interviewed many M&A reps, and during the interviews, I asked if they had ever represented a female or minority-owned startup. The answers were very telling. We had one older white guy whose firm had 100 percent white guys on the team. The only diversity was age, and their advisory board was 100 percent male, except for one Asian-American guy. When I asked about their experience and how we could trust that they could represent a female and minority-owned startup in this environment, the M&A specialist laughed and laughed nervously. Roz and I did not laugh. When he was finished laughing, he said, "It's never even occurred to me that would matter." We didn't go with that firm.

Sometimes, negotiations can become intense, even acrimonious. Some large acquiring companies can take on bullying tactics as a strategy, and you need someone who will stick up for you and not back down.

Once you've signed with your M&A lead, that person will start to create an organized system to approach and dialog with potential acquirers. Hopefully, you'll get nibbles and take some meetings with the potential acquirers. The M&A rep serves as a go-between and talks with you and them before and after the meetings. If things get more serious, beyond flirtation to thinking about making an offer, you head into due diligence.

YOU ARE NOW WOLVERINE: DUE DILIGENCE

Due diligence is the process by which the acquiring company can understand your entire operation, not just sales and contracts but your team, business practices, software, hardware, every aspect of the business before you reach the point of formally signing an agreement. The negotiations can all fall apart in due diligence, as something might come to light that invalidates the sale in the mind of the acquirer. The process is fraught with risk and so painful that—like childbirth—one naturally tries to forget it as soon as possible after it's over. There will be more documents and spreadsheets than you thought possible.

You don't want to enter due diligence unless you feel confident this deal is real. In rare cases, some big companies use due diligence as a form of oppositional research. They want to learn as much as they can about what you're doing, how, and why and then just do it without buying you. Ask your M&A rep how to protect your business during the due diligence process, and make sure everyone signs a nondisclosure agreement before putting the cards on the table.

There are many different specific reasons why an acquirer might acquire you: for your technology, for your team, or for your clients. You'll get better insight into why they're interested by the places where they focus most in due diligence. Acquirers want to make sure the technology is what you say it is, that you have relationships and contracts in place. We had to make sure we had everything buttoned down, especially with suppliers and vendors in order to convince Blackbaud we had everything they needed to move forward.

The whole process felt like Wolverine's flashbacks as his body is tortured into becoming a superhero. It's a terrifying, disorienting, writhing-in-unimaginable-pain nightmare but worth getting through to give your startup a whole new day and future potential.

NEGOTIATE FOR THE TEAM

While you may think your genius lies in your technology, in some cases, acquirers are less interested in the technology and more interested in the team. Strong engineers and developers who are doing cutting-edge innovation are not easy to find. The average tenure of any technology worker is eighteen months inside a company. You're lucky if you can keep them longer than that. I have a pretty good track record of being able to keep people on at least twice that amount of time, but not without effort on my part. A company may be interested in acquiring your team primarily to build out their own bench.

"For me, it's all about the culture. I think the biggest mistake anyone can make is not focusing enough on culture integration. This includes everything from the tone and content of the initial communications to how you transition the brand internally over time. You have to respect the culture of the company you are acquiring and recognize that you will need to create a new culture with both organizations. One organizational culture can't just eat the other one."

—CATHERINE LACOUR, CMO OF BLACKBAUD

Part of the negotiation is for your team. The acquirer normally asks people to sign on for eighteen months to four years, depending on the terms of the negotiation, because they want people to stay. Acquisition agreements often have a clause that defines a set period of time when the acquirer knows they'll have access to the team. If the acquirer doesn't want the whole team (for example, redundancies often occur with sales or customer success employees), you want to do what you can to protect your team. These are people who took a big chance on you.

They could have worked anywhere. Instead, they chose to support and build the dream of your product or service together with you. It's up to you to fight for them, to fight to make sure that they're going to benefit in some way from having joined forces with you.

WHERE DID YOU LAND?

Within getting acquired, the most common exit (after failure), there are four options. The low end is maintaining your dignity. This exit strategy cries, "No harm, no foul." You and your investors don't receive a lot in the transaction, but you also don't give much up, and you get a cool new job. Your technology might live on in some form within the new company. It's also known as "acqhire."

Beyond maintaining your dignity, the other levels are a new car, new house, and never having to work again for the rest of your life. Each in their own way are great options. You can say, "Look, we had a product. We built it into something. Somebody saw the promise of this, and we were able to hand the baton to a larger entity who could take it to the next length." You get to see your baby grow up.

AFTERMATH: TRANSITIONING TO A NEW POST-ACQUISITION WORLD

Going from running your own small crew to merging

into a much larger and more complex organization can be challenging, teeth-gnashing, frustrating, confusing, or all of the above. We worked very closely with the team at Blackbaud to achieve the smoothest possible integration of our company, Attentive.ly, into a giant corporation. Roz and I were most concerned about making sure our team was positioned to be successful no matter where they ended up within the company and ensuring our product got the resources it needed to continue its growth trajectory. I continued my conversation with Kevin McDearis, who was instrumental in helping Attentive.ly integrate successfully with Blackbaud, and asked him what makes the difference in terms of a successful acquisition for all involved in his experience. He gave me the following tips for triumph for founders to rock their merger:

- Seek advice from those who preceded you. Reach out to founders from prior acquisitions who are still with the company and have a reputation and proven track record for success.
- Understand the desired outcomes for the acquisition as defined by the acquiring company and then get to know those who will be instrumental in achieving those outcomes. In many cases that means learning the business so you can find those stakeholders.
- Identify and request the right executive sponsor who can provide advice, insights, and intercede on your behalf when needed.

Blackbaud has done many acquisitions over the years as a NASDAQ company. You'll find in strong companies that deciding on acquisitions is a team effort, which is why it can take six to twelve months from initial tease to signing the papers. Rachel Hutchisson is VP of Corporate Citizenship and Philanthropy at Blackbaud and someone I really look up to in my field of cause-driven tech. She said on this subject:

> Coming from the perspective of having been involved with twenty plus acquisitions on the acquiring end (and heavily involved in at least half of these), this would be my advice to founders on the threshold of acquisition....
>
> Looking back at the many acquisitions I've been involved with, I've come to see a lesson that people just starting out should know going in. Your startup was bought because it offers something special, some potential to scale within the larger organization. No kidding! But in trying to minimize disruption and keep people happy who might be excited but also wary about what's ahead, there's often a tendency to play down how much things will change. Guess what? Things WILL change. You know that. So embrace it and make sure you're really open with the team that the road ahead is going to be different even if it doesn't look like it right away.
>
> And as the leader of the startup that's been acquired, make

sure you're front and center, being human with your people who, although they may have known and wanted the deal to happen, are going to feel like they're in an alternate reality for a while. Some will love what's happening. Others will not. And it's important for you to stay connected with them, giving them an outlet to work through the many powerful emotions that can surface surrounding a deal. The change that's coming will unfold over time, and some of your people will be a part of it. Others will move on. The more human you are with each person, the better chance you have to work through what, when left to linger, can be very disruptive emotions while maintaining that much-needed focus on the business of your startup, which has to keep moving in order to deliver that purchaser of the very value they just bought.

RETURN ON INVESTMENT

At the time of the IPO or acquisition, the investor finally realizes their return on investment. It's a big moment for everybody and is a supernova burnout moment for many founders.

Startups are an emotional roller coaster. You've worked for almost a decade to reach this point, and when the acquisition papers are signed, you may have a "Now what?" moment. There's a flurry of activity that comes after the acquisition—meeting new people, blending with a new team, creating new teams—yet at some point you take a step back to look around from the mountain you've climbed. Everything looks different from up there.

The supernova moment is a good problem to have. Take the time to reassess and regather your strength. Even if you don't go supernova in the good way, you have still climbed a mountain. There might be a crater at the top of that mountain where your hopes and dreams were, but you've still climbed a mountain. Take a minute to look around and see how far you've come.

FAIL IS NOT A FOUR-LETTER WORD

We've talked about the best possible options. Your company goes public, and you become one of the wealthiest people in the world, or your company is acquired, and you get something from the bargain.

The sad truth for most startups is you're probably just going to go out of business. You reach the end of your business life cycle. It doesn't work out the way that you hoped, and that's okay. Women and minorities tend to be risk-averse because risk carries a higher price for them, real or perceived. They might not consider being a founder or joining a startup because the perceived risk seems high. They worry people will see them differently if the startup fails. They worry they will be tarnished in the marketplace and unable to get a job. Instead, the risk can bring a return even if your company fails. Even if you had to exit the hard way, it can and should be seen as a career booster.

If you have run a startup, most employers won't see an unsuccessful exit as a complete failure. What they see is someone who was brave, took a risk, managed to run a company for a period of time, and displayed a lot of executive function. They see a leader. They see someone who has been through the fire and held their head up high when they came out the other side. They see someone who has learned a lot in a short period of time.

"Never let the idea of failure deter you from realizing your vision or limit how big your vision can be. There were definitely people who thought that we might fail or didn't understand what Steph and I were planning to create with Away, and that's bound to happen, but I'm so glad that we ignored anyone who doubted us and focused on surrounding ourselves with people who believed in and supported our vision."

—JEN RUBIO, COFOUNDER AND CHIEF
BRAND OFFICER OF AWAY

The next step is something white men have perfected. This is your opportunity to #failup. Your story is not, "I failed." Your story is, "I tried something bold and experi-

mental. It didn't work out the way I'd hoped. Here's why."
Sophisticated employers understand it's not all your fault.
Environmental factors, including just being too early, play
a huge part in your success or lack thereof. Having a great
idea when the market isn't ready doesn't mean your idea
isn't brilliant. It means people aren't there yet.

You're now qualified for a much higher level of leadership within any given organization, and you should see
yourself that way. Talk about yourself that way. Describe
yourself that way on your résumé and LinkedIn profile.
You have to embody your story and declare, "I dared and I
dreamed, and here I am, ready for more." You can provide
fresh leadership and fresh ideas to a larger organization
and then be an intrapreneur inside an organization. You
bring what you learned about entrepreneurship to help
the large company stay on the cutting edge and continue
to integrate.

SPEEDBUMP

Again, the main speedbump is time. It may take you
longer to get acquired. During negotiations, don't let your
team be devalued because of the color of their skin or
their gender. If your team is mostly women and minorities, you need to make sure you highlight the strengths
of your team and what they bring to the table and crack
any unspoken or unconscious bias that can impact the

transaction head-on. The good news is companies are beginning to value diversity in and of itself. We work with people all the time, and the fact that we had a mostly female development team and a female CTO was attractive to many of the acquirers that we talked to. Unfortunately, not everyone is going to see it that way.

INVESTOR EYE-OPENER

Investors must encourage and support diversity in tech startups and understand that early-stage companies are going to need more support if the founder is black or brown. Your offer of resources could unlock a new potential. The exciting part about choosing to diversify your investments by working with women, minorities, and minority women, is that you can actually make an even bigger impact sometimes with that entrepreneur.

CONCLUSION

YOUR MOMMA IS PROUD OF YOU

When I mentioned to a friend of mine that I was writing this book, she said, "You know, Cheryl, more people have been to the moon than black woman who have successfully exited from their tech startups to date." There are hills left to climb. Success is going to look different depending on your journey and your trajectory. No matter what happens, being an entrepreneur, you've already succeeded. Just by seeing yourself in that context of, "I have a great idea, and I believe that I can be a leader and bring something new to the world," you have already been successful. Your momma is already proud of you. That's the good news.

You probably have fuzzy ideas about what success looks like as you think about your idea. The important thing is to position yourself to make decisions that help you achieve what you believe to be success.

Success may show up for you in different ways.

Success might look like hiring or doubling your staff. It might be getting that first funding check. It could be when you launch your website for the first time and you hang your shingle out there. Success might look like acquisition or an IPO.

Or success might look like going out of business and making the tough decision that you've gone as far as you could go.

"A LOT of crap will happen, a lot of things will happen that will make you think you can't go on or that you don't have what it takes or that you will never be good enough or that you should do what others tell you to do, but believe in yourself and follow what is the next right move for YOU. If you fail, you learn. If you slip, pick yourself up. Just keep going. Entrepreneurship is about having the resolve, the persistence, the character, and the perseverance you need to never, ever, ever, ever give up. If you believe in yourself, are willing to work hard, and never give up, you will succeed despite the critics, naysayers, haters, and everything else in between. Just decide to believe and to never give up. Know you can be the greatest and achieve anything you want, if you put your mind to it.

The best advice was just to trust myself more, listen to my instincts more, and put myself out there—meaning promote my company and myself—despite feeling imposter syndrome, not ready, etc., etc. Just going for it has allowed me to start living my best life and to feel an inner joy and peace within myself along the way."

—ASHLEY M. WILLIAMS, FOUNDER AND CEO OF RIZZARR

That's still success. You dared. You dreamed. You went out on a limb. You took a big risk. You decided to become a leader and take destiny into your own hands. Everyone is going to respect that, and you should not walk away feeling like a failure.

ROZ OFFERS WORDS OF ENCOURAGEMENT

As long as you're trying and learning from your setbacks, you're on the path to success. That's not just a cliché, it's science! A 2006 Harvard study showed entrepreneurs who "failed in a prior venture"[16] are more likely to succeed than first-time entrepreneurs. They're also more likely to get early-stage funding the second (or third, or fourth) time around. And once you've established a track record of success, your chances of future success increase even more. So if your first ride on the mechanical bull throws you: dust off and climb back on. You've got this!

16 Paul Gompers, Anna Kovner, Josh Lerner, David Scharfstein, Skill vs. Luck in Entrepreneurship and Venture Capital: Evidence from Serial Entrepreneurs, Working paper, Harvard University, July 2006.

Yeehaw!

Don't imagine you can do this on your own. Even if you are the primary owner, it takes a village to raise a company. Find your village. They're going to be not only investors but also customers, vendors, and teams that you might recruit. You're going to have different people, and you want different people attracted to your company, whether they be customers, investors, staff, or employees. Make sure that you are providing diversity and inclusion, that you're demonstrating that. Other people will look for that.

"Wish someone would have told me that some relationships will NOT survive entrepreneurship. And that is a BONUS! Not everyone is happy for you or believes that you can achieve your dreams. In fact, their negativity will sabotage you VICIOUSLY! Get the hell away from them and suffer no guilt about it."

—VIOLA LLEWELLYN, COFOUNDER OF OVAMBA

If you enjoyed this book and learned from it, hand it to someone else in your life who should read it. Nontraditional, black, brown, red, yellow, white, LGBTQ women and men need to stick together. The more people who know what's possible, the greater variety and wealth of products, apps, and services that solve real problems for people we'll have in the world.

Great ideas can come from anywhere and anyone. My hope is this book encourages you, especially if you may not think a startup is possible for you. I hope it gives you new courage and new resources with which to realize your dreams and the dreams of others.

ACKNOWLEDGMENTS

My story isn't possible without the help of my family, especially my mother Carmen Contee, my brother Clarence Contee, Jr., and my son Colm. I'd like to thank my friends and family around the world for your support and well-wishes over the years.

Many thanks to Roz Lemieux for all her contributions to my life and to this book. I want to give a special shout-out to the Attentive.ly team: Cynthia "Cindy" Mottershead, Jordyn Bonds, Lizzie Schaffer, Jeanette Russell, Jamie Mueller, Sam Marx, Charity Leschinski, Rose Whipple, Nick Darling, Candace Cross, Artie Patel, and Brandon Russell.

Attentive.ly's investors and advisors were true angels who believed in us when most others didn't. A special warm THANK YOU to Josh Mailman, Christopher Bentley, and Serious Change, Drew Bernard, Kesha Cash, Robin Klemm, Ph.D. and Christopher Klemm, Ph.D., Clarence Contee, Jr., Dan King, Daniel Weise, Dirk Wiggins, Eric Tumperi, Fran Sussner Rodgers and Charles Rodgers, Gene Chayevsky, Jonathan Brickman, Kristin Hull and Sarah Story, Marie Jorajuria, Matthew Palevsky, Mike Becker, Mike Shutt, Murray Goldman, Priya Bhikha and Jagruti Bhika, Sandor Straus, Joseph Thurakal, Thomas Roberts, Tom Kingsley, Victor Liu, Wayne Jordan and Quinn Delaney, New Media Ventures, and Atlanta Technology Angels.

Several other people acted as amazing advisors during our journey. Roz and I would like to thank Christie George, Julie Menter, Shannon Baker, Michael Horten, Tricia Salinero, Rajneesh Aggarwal, Bernie Dixon, Bill Hobbs, Scott Shaul, Dr. Timothy Dukes and Sally Dukes, and Dave Liloia.

So much gratitude to all those who provided quotes for this book. Your generously shared insights and life experiences gave the ideas in this book life! Many thanks to Drew Bernard, Anil Dash, Marla Blow, Viola Llewellyn, Kathryn Finney, Brandon Silverman, Sheena Allen, James Slezak, Stephanie Lampkin, Monique Woodard, Jen Rubio, Kesha Cash, Jeanette Russell, Charlene Li, Jewel Burks, Max Slavkin, Aaron Samuels, Heather Gold, Christie George, Josh Mailman, Lauren Maillian, Betsy

Hoover, Morgan Simon, Bee Chang Shapiro, Ariane Gold-man, Joseph Thurakal, Elisa Camahort Page, Ashley M. Willams, Tricia Salinero, Kevin McDearis, Christie Chiri-nos, Catherine LaCour, and Rachel Hutchisson.

We'd like to express maximum appreciation to the fol-lowing folks at Blackbaud, without whom the successful acquisition and integration of Attentive.ly into their company would not have been possible. Many thanks to Mark Davis, Brooke Huling, Rachel Simon, Jagtar Narula, Courtney Champion, Mary Beth Westmoreland, Jon Olson, Michael (Mike) Gianoni, and so many others.

I'd like to thank my partners and team at 270 Strategies and Do Big Things. Together, I know we can change the world for the better.

Finally—last but far from least—I'm so grateful for the team at Scribe Media, especially Barbara Boyd, Kather-ine Sears, Erin Tyler, Chelsea Vincent, and Zach Obront. This book simply would have remained a sparkle in my eye without their help and guidance. Thank you.

ABOUT THE AUTHOR

CHERYL CONTEE is the award-winning CEO and co-founder of Do Big Things, which brings together a diverse team that uses new narrative and new tech like blockchain, AI, bots and machine learning to make the world a better place for everyone.

Previously, she was the co-founder and CEO of Fission Strategy, which helped the world's leading nonprofits, foundations, and social enterprises design digital ecosystems that create change globally. She is also the co-founder of groundbreaking social marketing software Attentive.ly at Blackbaud, the first tech startup with a black female founder on board in history to be acquired by a NASDAQ-traded company. Cheryl is proud to be a co-founder of #YesWeCode, which represents the movement to help low-opportunity youth achieve high-quality tech careers. Her company Fission helped write the early source code for CrowdTangle, earning sweat equity in a successful social enterprise startup acquired by Facebook in December 2016.

Cheryl cofounded *Jack and Jill Politics*, writing as "Jill Tubman" on the leading top black audience targeted blog during the 2008 and 2012 election cycles. Cheryl has been listed among the "Influencers 50" in *Campaigns and Elections* magazine. Cheryl was named as an Affiliate of Harvard University's Berkman Center for Internet & Society. She was inducted into the first *Root 100* list of established and emerging African American leaders. *Huffington Post* included her as one of the "Top 27 Female Founders in Tech to Follow on Twitter" in 2011, as did *Black Enterprise*. *Fast Company* named her one of their "2010 Most Influential Women in Tech."

Cheryl has been featured in many media outlets including *Vanity Fair*, *Washington Post*, *New York Times*, *San Francisco Magazine*, C-SPAN, *Black Enterprise*, BBC, MSNBC, and CNN. She serves on several boards and advisory committees, including Citizen Engagement Lab and Digital Undivided, and was recently named the national board Chair for Netroots Nation. She received her BA from Yale University and has an International Executive MBA from Georgetown University. Cheryl's the proud parent of a rapidly growing little boy and lives with her family in the Bay Area.